STREAMING

IN

HEAVEN'S

FLOW

Kent Henry

This book and all other Kent Henry teaching materials, CD's and videos are available at KentHenry.com

ISBN 13: 9781490347752

Abbreviation Legion

AMP - The Amplified Bible
BBE - The Bible in Basic English
CJB - The Complete Jewish Bible
Con. - WJ Conybeare Pauline Epistles
HCS - Christian Standard Bible
DBY - The Darby Translation
ERV - Easy to Read Version
GEN - The Geneva Bible (1587)
GWD - God's Word Translation
HNV - Hebrew Names Version
KJV - King James Version
KNOX - The Knox Bible
LIT - Green's Literal Translation
MSG - The Message

NAS - New American Standard
NCV - New Century Version
NEB - The New English Bible
NKJV - New King James Version
NLV - New Life Bible
NLT - New Living Translation
Phi. - J.B. Phillips New Testament
REB - The Emphasized Bible
RHE - Douay-Rheims Bible
Tay. - Taylor Living Letters
TLB - The Living Bible
WNT - Weymouth New Testament
WYC - The Wycliffe Bible (1395)
YLT - Young's Literal Translation

Dedication

To my beautiful wife, Carla.

Proverbs 18:22 says, *"He who finds a wife finds a good thing and obtains favor from the LORD."* Well, I have much favor from the Lord because besides Jesus, Carla's love is the best thing that has touched my life.

Foreword

If you would have told pastors and church leaders in 1980 that in 20 years most of the body of Christ around the world would be singing similar church songs and responding to the Lord in worship in a similar way, people would have thought you were crazy!

By the year 2000 this had happened and is continuing to happen today. Kent Henry was a part of a small circle of voices that God used during those two decades to transform the church worship culture around the world.

Today there is a global surge of prayer where God is transforming His Bride once again, and Kent is a part of another group of forerunning messengers that are pointing a way forward for the Body of Christ.

"Streaming In Heaven's Flow" gives hope and a future for the church in worship and prayer before the Lord and champions what Jesus is doing in the earth today. Receive the message of this book, take the leap of faith and press into Jesus in a personal and corporate way, and your reward will be great in the kingdom of God.

Jim Stern - Lead Pastor *Destinychurch.org*

Introduction

Over thirty years ago, the Lord gave me this instruction:

"Kent, teach My Body how to

intermingle praise with prayer and
worship with intercession."

While processing through this word, several thoughts came to my mind. If God's people, who love to worship and love His presence ever learned to combine their worship with intercession, there would be explosive results for the greater glory of God.

The power of our praise joined with strong prayer is part of "Streaming in Heaven's Flow." The dynamics of worship, prayer and music triumph over the powers of darkness. When we join our worship directly to intercession, the plans and purposes of God are made more fully manifest in the earth.

One of my greatest dreams, one of my greatest desires is to see the majority of the American Church praying at a much higher level. I have been ministering on the road for over 30 years. On average, I have done 32 Worship Weekends a year during that time period. I have a fairly good idea of who the American Church is and what the American Church is not. I know for sure that prayerlessness is a major part of what is killing the American Church.

To be very clear, one of our greatest weaknesses is the lack of prayer, intercession, devotion to Jesus and deeper worship in both church leadership and the congregations themselves.

There is a Biblical fix to all of this. Pray more, Worship more. Not in a boring fashion but truly with the Holy Spirit's leadership and touch on it.

This is the time we must grow the devotional life of everyday believers, flowing in deeper worship and greater prayer. This is a high priority in the heart of the Lord. I know that there is exponential power available whenever we merge worship, prayer and music together.

Each chapter will unfold a powerful truth of how to activate yourself and other believers in higher grade prayer and worship.

Worship, prayer and music are "Built to Run Together," praise with prayer, worship with intercession. "Jesus is the Core of Everything" and our focus and attention should be daily on the worthy Lamb that was slain.

We are to help people see and understand the true value of the "Prayers of the Saints." This is God's people engaged in the priestly ministry of worship and intercession. The Lord thankfully interrupted me from making a "worker bee" book.

I could have had a book all about how to do prayer and worship but we must know deeply the true motivation of why we do it. "Because of Love." It is the chapter that unfolds the power of His love, our need for intimacy and encountering God.

This excellent truth of "Every Believer's Eternal Identity" helped our people cross over into the greater understanding of the culture of prayer and worship. It is way of life for those who are priests unto the Lord.

Of super importance in everything we are doing is "Singing and Praying the Word of God." God's Word will not return void or empty. So we center all that we do around the Bible. Hopefully we are sensing an urgency to get busy with Jesus in the ministry He is currently doing . . .
"He ever lives to make intercession (Hebrews 7:25). "

We must awaken . . .

"Take Heed, Watch and Pray."

Contents

Appendices

Built to Run Together

While in the worship realm,
all the borders are gone
and the enemy is forbidden
from stopping your heart and your voice
from yielding its full praise and worship.

Focused prayer riding on top
of the zeal of worship
is unstoppable.
Through the commitment of our hearts to it,
our prayers will be relentless.

Chapter One

Built to Run Together:

Praise with Prayer, Worship with Intercession

The Worship Realm:

John 4:23-24 True Worshippers Worship the Father
in Spirit and Truth

> [23] *"But an hour is coming, and now is, when **the true worshippers** will worship the Father in spirit and truth; for such people the Father seeks to be **His worshippers**.* [24] *God is spirit, and those who worship Him must **worship in spirit and truth**."*

The Prayer Realm:

Ephesians 6:18   Be Praying at all Times in the Spirit

> *Pray at all times in the Spirit, with all petition be praying, with all [manner of] entreaty. To that end, keep alert and watch with strong purpose and perseverance, interceding on behalf of all the saints.*   (AMP, NAS)

The Music Realm:

Isaiah 30:32   Anointed Music, a Tool and a Weapon

> *And every blow of the rod of punishment, which the LORD will lay on him [King of Assyria], will be **with the music** of [Israel's] tambourines and lyres; when in battle He attacks [Assyria], brandishing weapons, He will fight them.*
>   (NAS, AMP)
>
> *. . . He will beat them **to the music** of tambourines and harps; He will fight against them with His mighty weapons.*
>   (NCV)

Over thirty years ago, the Lord gave me this instruction: "Kent, teach My Body how to

intermingle praise with prayer and
worship with intercession."

While processing through this word, several thoughts came to my mind. If God's people, who love to worship and love His presence ever learned to combine their worship with intercession, there would be explosive results for the greater glory of God.

The power of our praise joined with strong prayer is part of "Streaming in Heaven's Flow." The power of worship, prayer and music triumph over the powers of darkness. When we join our worship directly to intercession, the plans and purposes of God are made more fully manifest in the earth.

In August of 1974, I started leading praise and worship for my youth group. I led worship for three different churches up through the year 1983. During this nine year period, I could not find any books on this topic of flowing in the Spirit, moving between worship and prayer and then back again.

I learned through experience about the power of **worship, prayer and music** that these are "built to run together." I understand now, this has been God's idea all along. What a tremendous trio we have in our arsenal to pray and do spiritual warfare.

Why would we do extended times of **worship** and not cross over into prayer while we are there in His presence?

Why would we ever want to **pray** without the power of anointed music supporting that prayer?

Why do we not have a greater understanding that **music** was created to glorify the Lord, to help us do worship and focused prayer?

700 Worshippers: What if They Prayed?

It was just three years ago, my youngest daughter, Ariel (she was 17 at the time) and I were headed to a major worship conference in Tennessee. We were delayed arriving on the first night because there was an accident on the highway. We were only ten minutes late and so we joined some of the most powerful worship I had been in for years. This is a very well known, young worship leader who took us deep in the Lord's presence. Then we went to even deeper places in worship. It was really a beautiful hour of being before the Throne.

Here's what crossed my mind though: with over 700 worshippers freely flowing in the presence of God, not one time of corporate prayer took place. There was no direction ever given from the platform for the whole group to enter into prayer or intercession.

The Lord's presence was there. The hearts of the people were there. We had spiritual tools and weapons available but we just didn't put them to use.

Just think: 700 worshippers moving straight into prayer, say for God's justice to be released in specific nations. We could have prayed for missionaries in those nations. We could have prayed against human sex-trade trafficking and the end of the taking of innocent lives, in abortion. You see the understanding of the power and value of corporate prayer is known and utilized by so few.

Romans 15:5-6

> [5] ... *be of the same mind with one another according to Christ Jesus,*
> [6] *so that with* **one accord** *you may with* **one voice** *glorify the God and Father of our Lord Jesus Christ.*

Back to My Personal Story

Years ago, through practical experience, I learned that as I was leading worship, we would begin "Streaming in Heaven's Flow." As this river increased in intensity, the presence of God would be released.

During these times, I would start praying and interceding about different things as they came up in my spirit. This is when I realized that intermingling praise with prayer and worship with intercession should be a larger part of our life.

4

Back then, there was very little explanation, revelation or teaching on the combination of worship, prayer and music. The Holy Spirit began helping us know the heart of our Father for the ministry of worship and prayer **fused together**. So we saw tremendous results from this combination.

Focused prayer riding on top
of the zeal of worship is unstoppable.
Through the commitment of
our hearts to it,
our prayers will be relentless.

While doing Worship Weekends on the road, people came with great excitement. Once we gathered and the music began, people moved deeper into the place of worship. You could tell they had shifted their focus from their needs and the busyness of their week over to flowing in the presence of God.

They began "**going vertical**,"
worship that is directed straight to the Lord.

It was during this time we could move right into prayer. As we moved into the **deeper realms** of worship, the depths of His presence would activate the "Spirit of prayer" in our hearts. As a result, intercession would break out. People entered into prayer, the music kept playing becoming the foundation for it.

Intercession, then, starts releasing the stored-up force of His Word while activating His power against the kingdom of darkness. This is where intercessory prayer has the **power to bind and loose** as Jesus said in Matthew 16:19. It's a part of our spiritual warfare that carries God's authority.

*And I will give you the **keys** of the **kingdom** of heaven, and whatever you **bind** on earth will be bound in heaven, and whatever you **loose** on earth will be loosed in heaven."* (NKJV)

Revelation 1:17-18

[17] *When I saw Him, I fell at His feet like a dead man. And He placed His right hand on me, saying, Do not be afraid; I am the first and the last,*

5

^{18} *and the living One; and I was dead, and behold, I am alive forevermore, and **I have the keys of death and of Hades.***

The Power of the Worship Realm

John 4:23-24   True Worshippers Worship in Spirit and Truth

^{23} *"But an hour is coming, and now is, when **the true worshippers** will worship the Father in spirit and truth; for such people the Father seeks to be **His worshippers**.*
^{24} *"God is spirit, and those who worship Him must **worship in spirit and truth**."*

We must not undervalue the power of human hearts engaged in true worship. This truly is one of the few realms where a person's spirit, soul and body stands at total attention toward the Lord Himself.

While in the worship realm,
all the borders are gone
and the enemy is forbidden
from stopping your heart and your voice
from yielding its full praise and worship.

Worship is the place where we soar with wings as eagles. The interplay between the Lord and one of His worshippers is so strong and yet so indefinable.

After leading worship for almost 40 years, the stories of the presence and grace of God changing hearts and lives are too numerous to number. We have seen miracles. We have seen angels ascending and descending. We have seen the river of God touch the hardest of hearts. This is why the worship realm deserves its own category.

As I have been doing conferences the last seven years, I have been opening general sessions and classes with this statement: "Worship is not enough!" The look on people's faces is real astonishment. I can tell that people are somewhat bewildered. How could someone like Kent Henry, who has led worship for so long, in so many places, for so many people, make such a statement?

Higher Revelation Has Come

It's because a **higher revelation has come**. If you're going to spend your time and energy in deep worship and the pursuit of God, then by all means, cross over into prayer and intercession. While you are there in His presence, you can pray effectively in this same anointing you are standing in.

If you go to the Throne Room and worship, you will receive a blessing. But if you go to the Throne Room and start praying out of your time of worship, you have accomplished two things. You have blessed the Father's heart but you have also uttered words that are damaging the kingdom of darkness.

Then you have begun fulfilling the **priestly ministry** of prayer and worship. When you pray and intercede, you join Jesus in His current ministry. He ever lives to make intercession.

That's why I say . . .

"Worship in and of itself is enough.
But on the other hand,
it's never enough until we are
intermingling praise with prayer and
worship with intercession."

The Power of the Prayer Realm

Ephesians 6:18

> *Pray at all times in the Spirit, with all petition be praying, with all [manner of] entreaty. To that end, keep alert and watch with strong purpose and perseverance, interceding in behalf of all the saints.* (AMP, NAS)

I found this scripture many years ago in my early 20's. I truly love every dimension of Ephesians 6:18. But I said to the Lord, "God, how do you expect me to fulfill this 'praying at all times'?" I felt overwhelmed at the largeness of this command.

It is then that He said to me, "It is impossible in your own flesh or your strength. But as you yield to My Holy Spirit you will be able to flow daily in praying at all times." My personality and my make up is such that I really love the challenge of these kinds of scriptures. I have learned to count more on the Holy Spirit's leadership and His direction as I go throughout my day, praying at all times.

When you take the realm of worship and prayer into a corporate setting inside of a **Prayer Room**,* the dynamic is mind-blowing.

Worship is going, hearts start flowing, prayer leaders praying and the singing and praying of God's Word begins. It releases the unction of the three realms: worship, prayer and music. It is where the strong anointing of His glory is experienced at the same time. Obviously, the music plays a huge part in creating a music bed, a stream for singers and prayer leaders to ride on.

* [The Prayer Room: I am referring to our church sanctuary (Destiny Church in St. Louis) where we run prayer and worship with live music and singers. We pray all day Tuesday, 9:00 a.m. until 8:30 p.m. So, the rest of the week, we have an additional 10 hours of "Worship, Prayer and Music" in prayer room sets. There are one hour Adoration sets, as well as 90 minute Intercession sets.]

You need to enter into to the fullness of your calling and destiny as Priests unto the Lord. You will know the endorsement of God as you pray and sing His Word.

This is the next realm most believers should be moving into. This is also why the enemy has attempted to shut us down in prayer and worship. The scheme of the enemy is to keep these three realms separate or locked up under the spirit of man's control.

Pray More, Worship More

When you begin to see the power of corporate prayer, worship, and music as God created them, you never want to stop doing any of the three. Pray more, worship more. Pray more, worship more. And when you are finished with that, pray more, and worship more. For where the Spirit of the Lord is, there is liberty.

2Corinthians 3:17

> *Now the Lord is the Spirit, and where the Spirit of the Lord is, there is liberty.*

> *Now the Lord is the Spirit, and where the Spirit of the Lord is, there is liberty (emancipation from bondage, freedom).*
> (AMP)

> *The heart is free where the Spirit of the Lord is.* (NLV)

The Message Bible translates 2 Corinthians 3:17 this way in contemporary language.

> *They suddenly (the children of Israel) recognize that God, (He) is a **living, personal presence**, not a piece of chiseled stone.*

> *And when God is personally present, a living Spirit, that old, constricting legislation is recognized as obsolete. We're free of it!* (MSG)

Think about what this scripture is revealing. Religious people turn God into their own religious image. They try to invalidate the Word and ways of God with their made-up traditions, people jumping through hoops, "making constrictive legislation" to rule over the lives of men and women. The Lord is not for this. He is against it.

Many church leaders find it very difficult to get by engaging the spirit of control to control the flow of their church meetings.

The Prayer Room by its nature avoids the need to do these kind of things. It's hearts united with fire, to sing and pray the Word at the highest levels.

To me, it's a wonderful throw back to my early days of ministry. These were gatherings where the Holy Spirit led and where the presence of God was unrestricted. The fruit of these services: "hundreds got saved and thousands were changed."

The Power of the Music Realm

Isaiah 30:32   Anointed Music, a Tool and a Weapon

> *And every blow of the rod of punishment, which the LORD will lay on him [King of Assyria], will be **with the music** of [Israel's]*

9

tambourines and lyres; when in battle He attacks [Assyria], brandishing weapons, He will fight them. (NAS, AMP)
. . . He will beat them **to the music** *of tambourines and harps; He will fight against them with His mighty weapons.* (NCV)

Because of the wonderful music gifts the Lord has given me from my mother's womb, the music realm is one of my personal favorites.

It is so exciting to have first hand knowledge and experience of how music touches the heart of God and the heart of man. God created music and the devil (Lucifer) did not. The devil tries to distort and misuse the things that God has created for our help and His glory.

There are so many people that have totally ditched their singing or music gift because of a lack of appreciation or encouragement and just shear burn out. Music is for joy and therapy. Singing is for lifting up and refreshment. The Prayer Room is a perfect solution for you if you've hit the wall and laid your singing/music gifts aside.

It's a place where there is no pressure, there are not very many people, and it's not performance based. Singing and music in the prayer room is "Presence based." It's not about doing it for people, it's about doing it to the Lord.

God created music with its own anointing that can sooth the savage soul and heal the brokenhearted.

Please consider this, you should start singing and playing music again. Pick up your instrument and start playing again. Music is for stirring your soul, releasing your creativity. All the while you worship and pray, music by its very nature is so freeing to the human heart.

I have grown weary through the years of those that try to regulate it. Those that use it for all the wrong intentions. Those that use music even in church circles for their own gain. It's time to . . . STOP IT!

Presence Based as Opposed to Performance Driven

Passionate music that flows from consecrated hearts is "the bomb." It is also the "balm," the ointment or the oil for healing. The first one blows stuff up and the second releases healing power. When we choose to use music to create the foundation for worship and prayer, there is no higher purpose for music.

That's why this trio, rolled up together and functioning in one accord, releases Heavenly power on this unclean earth. Even though the fight for the music that glorifies God has gone on for thousands of years, our choice is to use music and worship to honor the Lord and to defeat the darkness.

Our prayers and worship rise as incense before the Lord. It's clearly defined in Revelation 5 verse 8:

"When He had taken the scroll, the four living creatures and the twenty-four elders fell down before the Lamb,

> *each one holding a harp and*
> *golden bowls **full of incense**,*
> *which are the **prayers of the saints**."*

We present ourselves as a living sacrifices which is our spiritual service of worship, while diligent worship and prayer rises as incense.

The Lord does take notice. These prayers are stored as incense and not one of them is forgotten.

Romans12:1

Therefore I urge you [I appeal to you], brethren, [in view of all] the mercies of God,

[to make a decisive dedication] to present your bodies a living and holy sacrifice, acceptable [well-pleasing] to God, which is your spiritual service of worship. (NAS, AMP)

At Destiny Church, I am one of the recruiters for finding new singers and musicians as they come and visit our Prayer Room. I have run into so many people who have been talked out of using their gifts because of whatever.

Once you see young teenagers learning to sing and play their instruments in a Presence-based Prayer Room, it's totally fulfilling. It is one of the best situations in which to learn. This is what is beautiful.

This is what is truly delightful; seeing the revelation of the glory of God hit the kids sometime during their time of ministering to the Lord.

The kids are never the same. When teenagers find this place, they love it and they get it. They quickly understand the value and the dynamic of music, of their playing and singing; especially how the Lord receives glory from it.

Every church should be intentionally locating the core group teenagers of their youth group and helping them grow their spiritual life and their music gift to the next level.

The Place of Refreshing, Cleansing and Recovery

Acts 3:19

> *Therefore repent and return, so that your sins may be wiped away, in order that times of refreshing may come from the presence of the Lord;*
>
> *... that times of refreshing (recovering from the effects of heat, of **reviving with fresh air**) come from the presence of the Lord.*
> (AMP)

This is one of my all time favorite New Testament scriptures. This is the promise of Almighty God that if you repent and return to Him, regardless of what you have done, He forgives your sin. Then He releases the times of refreshing that come from His presence, that come from Him personally.

Again, extended times of prayer and worship keep you fresh in the Holy Spirit and keeps the flame of the Lord burning at a higher level. As refreshing comes upon you, your heart is more open to the cleansing rain of the Lord.

Walking with a pure conscience is such a free state for every believer. Staying in a cleansed place, walking with clean hands and a pure heart makes us strong in the Lord and in the power of His might.

Times of refreshing and cleansing
lead to the place of full recovery.
Your spiritual equilibrium (balance)
stays fine tuned with regular
sustained times of prayer and worship.

Single-Hearted Devotion to Christ

As much as I love Sunday morning services, many times there is not much place for effective prayer during those services. Also, the time and depth of worship has also become very limited.

Because of a lack of spiritual encounters with God, many Christians are a half inch deep and a mile wide in their walk with the Lord. This is not a good thing. There has been an absence of the development of a true devotional life of worship and prayer to Christ.

Paul warned the Corinthian people in his second letter to them. [Remember, the Corinthian believers were those who were known for walking in the power gifts.]

2Corinthians 11:3

> *"But I am afraid that, as the serpent deceived Eve by his craftiness, your minds will be led astray from the **simplicity** and **purity** of **devotion** to Christ."*

> *... so your minds may be led astray from their **single-heartedness** and their **fidelity** to Christ.* (WNT)

> *But I have a fear, that in some way, as Eve was tricked by the deceit of the snake, your minds may be turned away from their simple and **holy love** for Christ.* (BBE)

> *... so your minds may be corrupted and seduced from **wholehearted, sincere** and **pure devotion** to Christ.* (AMP)

How are we currently growing the devotional lives of everyday believers to a deeper level toward Christ? Most churches have done away with special gatherings like: nights of worship, times of prayer and fasting, meetings set aside just to

13

seek the Lord for greater light and revelation. How can we expect people to be more spiritual when we have cut out the very meetings that would help them be more spiritual?

This is why our senior leader, Jim Stern, and the leadership team chose the Prayer Room atmosphere and environment. It helps people encounter the Lord at the highest levels while they are actively doing prayer and worship.

Even after all my years of experience, I find it the best place for the activation of spiritual gifts and the development of singing and music abilities.

Growing Greater Love and Devotion to Jesus

Our prayer room at Destiny Church in St Louis has lengthened and deepened the commitment of hundreds of people that were mostly "outer court" believers.

They would come to church two or three times a month. They would try to enter into the thirty or forty minutes of worship which was hard for them to do. The reason for this was their week consisted of very little Bible study or worship time.

"Streaming in Heaven's Flow" of worship, prayer and music has helped people grow their devotional lives. As we pray during a 90 minute intercession set, there are two twenty minute prayer cycles that happen during this time.

So our singers, musicians and prayer leaders are making spiritual level jumps because they are navigating through extended times of prayer and worship. So the light of His Word and the revelation of the Father's heart becomes more readily apparent.

The combining of worship, prayer and music as the triple threat anointing helps people mature in the things of the Spirit. This has been God's intention all along.

Every pastor and leader has a huge responsibility. And that responsibility is to grow the devotional life of the core group of their church. We are helping every member to a place of greater love and devotion to Jesus. We have found that doing the Prayer Room together is an effective way to do this.

God's Intention all Along

The heart of a human being, worshipping and adoring the Lord has much power on it. The function of worship is to give God His glory and recognize His worth in light of who He is and what He does.

But very few people have ever analyzed the outcome of intense times of being before the Lord. There are many things that happen to and through a person during times of intimate worship and passionate prayer. Some of the results are:

1. The power of pure worship used at the highest level is like the Refiners Fire that keeps our hearts pure and our mind focused on the Lord.

2. The knowledge of who God is and what He does has become more deeply set in our hearts.

3. Our people are stronger in their ability to get in and flow in worship and prayer. They have become like toned athletes or runners that can go a long time before becoming weary.

4. Our spiritual discernment has grown and runs at a higher level.

5. As we have been faithful to do extended times in the Prayer Room, our eyes and hearts have been opened to some of the deeper things of the Word of God and His ways.

6. The sense of unity and one accord is much stronger. Our church and the prayer and worship community within it, have come together in a greater way.

We must keep these things in mind always.

❖ Jesus is **the core** of everything that we are doing.

❖ We are becoming more active in prayer and worship because of love. Because He first loved us we can love Him in heart and deed.

❖ There is a coming revelation of every believers eternal identity. It is going to be highly known and understood that . . .

- Priesthood and priestly ministry is our eternal identity.

- Clouds of incense will be consistently rising before the Lord and over our cities because of the prayers of the Saints.

- We will truly know that the weapons of our spiritual warfare, they are surely not carnal or fleshly. But they are mighty through God to the pulling down of strongholds.

- Prayer and worship is the mission and the mandate that we are carrying out through our everyday lifestyle.

We are seeing the greater things of His kingdom accomplished while interceding for His will to become preeminent in the earth. We realize now, that this has been in the forefront of God's heart all along. The Lord knew what the awesome flow of deep worship and passionate prayer would do to us.

Now we are sold on these times of deeper worship and prayer. They are essential for spiritual growth and doing the work of His priestly calling. After five years of consistent prayer and worship, we have proven this to our own hearts. Hopefully you can begin to see that the three realms of worship, prayer and music are very vital on so many fronts.

Streaming *in* *Heaven's* *Flow*

Built to Run Together:

Praise with Prayer, Worship with Intercession

The Worship Realm

John 4:23-24 True Worshippers Worship the Father in
Spirit and Truth

The Prayer Realm

Ephesians 6:18 Be Praying at all Times in the Spirit

The Music Realm

Isaiah 30:32 Anointed Music, a Tool and a Weapon

I. Intermingle Praise with Prayer and Worship with Intercession

If God's people, who love to worship and love His presence ever learned to combine their worship with intercession, there would be explosive results for the greater glory of God.

A. 700 Worshippers: What if They Had Prayed?

We had spiritual tools and weapons available but we just didn't put them to use.

Romans 15:6 ... *with one accord you may with one voice glorify the God and Father of our Lord Jesus Christ.*

B. Back to My Personal Story

Focused prayer riding on top of the zeal of worship is unstoppable. Through the commitment of our hearts to it, this prayer will be relentless.

II. The Power of the Worship Realm

While in the worship realm, all the borders are gone and the enemy is forbidden from stopping your heart and your voice from yielding its full praise and worship.

A. Higher Revelation Has Come

When you pray and intercede, you join Jesus in His current

ministry. He ever lives to make intercession.

(Hebrews 7:25)

III. The Power of the Prayer Realm

Ephesians 6:18 *Pray at all times in the Spirit . . .*

You need to enter into to the fullness of your calling and destiny as Priests unto the Lord.

A. Pray More, Worship More

When you begin to see the power of corporate prayer, worship, and music as God created them, you never want to stop doing any of the three.

IV. The Power of the Music Realm

Music is for joy and therapy. Singing is for lifting up and refreshment. The Prayer Room is a perfect solution for you.

A. Presence Based as Opposed to Performance Driven

We present ourselves as a living sacrifices which is our spiritual service of worship, while diligent worship and prayer rises as incense. Romans 12:1

B. The Place of Refreshing, Cleansing and Recovery

Acts 3:19 *. . . that times of refreshing may come from the presence of the Lord; . . . that times of refreshing (recovering from the effects of heat, of **reviving with fresh air**) come from the presence of the Lord.*

C. Single-Hearted Devotion to Christ

2Corinthians 11:3 *"But I am afraid that, as the serpent deceived Eve by his craftiness, your minds will be led astray from the **simplicity** and **purity** of **devotion** to Christ."*

D. Growing Greater Love and Devotion to Jesus

"Streaming in Heaven's Flow" of worship, prayer and music has helped people grow their devotional lives.
Jesus is **the core** of everything that we are doing.
Prayer and worship is the mission and the mandate.

Jesus Is the Core of Everything

*Simply beholding
a small portion of
Who He really is, is enough
to change us for a lifetime. And then
beyond our lifetime comes eternity.*

*Jesus
. . . the Master Lord over all spirits.
. . . His light in power dispels all darkness.
. . . His great grace is superior to the works of men.
. . . His justice triumphs over all wickedness.
. . . His redemption covers the fallen state of man.*

Chapter Two

Jesus Is The Core of Everything

Worthy is the Lamb that was Slain, He Made Us to Be a Kingdom of Priests

Revelation 5:6, 9-10

> [6] *And I saw in the middle of the throne and of the four living creatures*
> *and in the midst of the elders, stood a Lamb as it had **been slain** . . .* (NAS, KJV)
> [9] *And they (the four living creatures and the twenty-four elders) sang a new song, saying,*
>
> *"**Worthy** are You to take the scroll and to break its seals; for **You were slain**, and **purchased** for God **with Your blood***
> *men from every tribe and tongue and people and nation."*
>
> [10] *"You have made them to be a kingdom and **priests to our God**; and they will reign upon the earth."*

These scriptures are a large part of the revelation of the Person of the Lord Jesus. His greatness and His glory are revealed in them. His Lordship and authority is clearly defined. He is truly " . . . our Awesome God."

The Person of the Lord Jesus

Jesus was a real person who walked on the earth. The very being of the Son of God was here in human form and then returned to all of His glory. He is currently seen in Heaven in all of His awesomeness and all of His beauty but now with a glorified body that has scars on it.

This Jesus is beautiful beyond all description. He is stunning. He is glorious. He is overwhelming. This is why **Jesus has to be the core** of everything that we are doing and that we are all about.

Our churches, our teachers and preachers have greatly limited their teaching on Jesus, in general. But most have almost never taught the character and the attributes of the resurrected Person of the Lord Jesus as He is in Heaven right now.

I have such a hunger to know Him and how He functions in His current resurrected state. Theologians and Bible students spend years studying about Jesus as He walked through His earthly ministry. This is important and does reveal much of His character, His heart and the reason that He came to earth.

But we must also deeply search the Word of God for this Heavenly realm of His life, the Ascended, Resurrected Redeemer of all the earth.

We should be in constant pursuit of the knowledge of Who He is, and what He does now and the ministry He is currently doing.

Hebrews 7:25 tells us, "He ever lives now to make intercession for you and me" and I believe He speaks over the purposes and mission of the Father concerning the redemption of the earth.

The Amplified Bible puts it this way . . . "since He (Jesus) is always living to make petition to God for them (He has saved) and intercede with God and intervene for them."

Revelation 5:6, 9-10 tells us some of the most powerful revelations that we **must** know about Jesus:

Who He is and **what** He has done and what He is doing right now.

This chapter of the book of Revelation also gives us insight unto the Heavenly model of worship, prayer and music. It is the reason for the title of this book, "Streaming in Heaven's Flow."

Our Foundational Need is to Know These Three Points

First, **Who** is it that Heaven sees?

Second, **what** is it that Heaven knows?

Third, **how** then does Heaven respond?

These three points are the base line for the heart and theology of prayer and worship; understanding why we would commit our lives and time to diligent prayer and worship.

First, Who is it that Heaven sees?

Jesus, the Lamb of God, slain

It is **Jesus**, the slain Lamb of God.

Revelation 5:6

*I saw in the middle of the high seat (of the throne), a Lamb in His place, which seemed as if it had been **put to death**...* (BBE)

*He looked as if He had been **offered in sacrifice**,* (WNT)

*... showing that it (the Lamb) had been slain (**slaughtered**, killed);* (CJB, REB, GEN)

The Father, Holy Spirit, the four living creatures and all the angels had for all eternity seen Jesus in all of His Glory. They are seeing Him now, in all of His restored power, sitting on His Throne in His splendor and magnificence.

In trying to help people understand the vastness of the presence of God while teaching, I had this thought. If the Lord were a thousand faceted diamond ring, it would speak volumes about His glory and His beauty.

But if there were a thousand facets additionally in every facet of the first thousand and so on, we would be seeing a picture of the ever unfolding presence, greatness and beauty of the Lord.

Many Bible commentators give the reason why the four living creatures and the seraphim angels keep crying "holy." It is because they are seeing another facet of the Person of the Lord unveiled before their eyes. They are discovering the fullness of

His Person and His beauty as it is ongoing and forever being revealed.

Because He is worthy,
He could break the seals on the scroll
releasing the stored-up plans
and the government of God
so they could go forth.

There was only one found worthy to break the seals on the scroll and look into it - JESUS. (Revelation 5:9)

Because of His sacrifice, His suffering on the Cross, His total obedience to the will of the Father even unto death, He is found worthy.

Beholding Who Jesus Is

Simply beholding a small portion of Who He really is, is enough to change us for a lifetime. And then beyond our lifetime comes eternity. After the second coming of Christ, in eternity and the millennial reign of the King of Glory, in and over New Jerusalem, we will understand Who Jesus is. So many believers have missed this profound truth.

The reason we must pursue higher levels of devotion, worship and Bible study is that within them are found the revelation of the Son of God. It will take dedicated, additional amounts of time to even scratch the surface to know of the revelation of the Lord Jesus.

We have certainly underplayed the importance of Jesus because of our self-centeredness. The fact is, our thoughts and our actions revolve way too much around us. It includes our focus on how our life is doing and where our life should be going.

An Example of Dedication and Devotion

I remember the first time that I heard about the Cloistered Nuns as a religious order. A nun is a member of a religious community of women, living under vows of poverty, chastity, and obedience. They are women who decided to dedicate their life to serving the Lord within the four walls of their convent or monastery. They voluntarily choose to leave mainstream society to be in a place of seclusion unto the Lord. They live their life in prayer and contemplation.

I attended a Catholic grade school growing up. The Cloistered Nuns made an impression on me because of their dedication and devotion to Jesus. These ladies chose a whole different lifestyle. They chose not to be married in the natural so that they would be married to the Lord. They chose not to have babies in the natural that they may pray for the children of the world to know the Lamb of God.

I had the Lord speak to me three years ago while I was sitting in the Prayer Room at Destiny Church. I clearly heard Him say to my heart, "Kent, I want you to live monastically before Me." My first thought was living a lifestyle like the monks that are in a monastery.

And I responded, "Lord how would You intend for me to do this since I am already married and have three children. Two of my children are already married. And furthermore, I have three grandchildren on top of it all." And He responded in turn, "Take some of your irons out of the fire, take some things off of your plate. You are way **too busy** to live a deeper life of devotion unto Me."

Every believer needs to live some part of their life in dedicated times of deeper devotion to Him, to know His ways and know Him intimately.

To the point: every believer needs to live part of their life like the cloistered nuns. We owe the Lord dedicated times of deeper devotion to know Him and His ways intimately. I want to be clear. I am in fulltime ministry. I have been for 39 years. I actually make my living by singing, playing worship music, preaching and teaching Worship Prayer Weekends.

While most people have 9-5 jobs and are married with one or two children, they have super busy lives. But each one of us has unrestricted times that we could devote to knowing the Lord better. The time of meditation and study of God's Word are usually the first things to go in our busy schedule.

We should begin with simple morning prayer times and prayers that touch the heart of God. Even during our church attendance there is very little prayer associated with those services. These meetings were originally built around the Person of the Lord Jesus but that has greatly changed as well.

I am saying to you, "take some irons out of the fire, remove some things off of your plate and press into the Lord." There are greater depths of His presence awaiting us all.

You Are Worthy of It All

Revelation 4:11

> *Thou art **worthy**, O Lord, to receive glory and honor and power: for Thou hast created **all** things,*
> > *and **for Thy pleasure** they are and were created.* (KJV)

> *"Our Lord and our God, it is **right for You** to have the*
> > ***shining-greatness** and the honor and the power.*
> *You made all things. They were made and have life because*
> > *You wanted it that way."* (NLV)

> *"Our Lord and God, **You deserve** to receive glory, honor, and power because You created everything."* (GWD)

> *... saying, "It is **fitting**, O our Lord and God, that we should ascribe unto Thee the glory and the honor and the power."*
> > (WNT)

There is a song we are currently using in our Prayer Room that has become a major blessing along with a dynamic revelation. The song is by David Brymer. It is easily located on You Tube by its' title, "Worthy of it All."

The Chorus goes like this:

> "You are worthy of it all, You are worthy of it all,
> For from You are all things, to You are all things.
> You deserve the Glory."

Then the verse declares part of Revelation 5:

"All the saints and angels bow before Your Throne,
All the elders cast their crowns before
the Lamb of God and sing."

Why do all the saints and angels bow before Jesus on the Throne? Why would the elders cast their crowns of respect and honor before the Lamb of God? Because He really is "worthy of it all!"

By peering into Heaven, we get a glimpse of the true glory and worth of the Son of God. It is time for us to take Heaven's example and do worship and prayer from the true perspective of how worthy Jesus really is.

We need to get our eyes off of us and our preoccupation with perfecting the music, because we are centered on being performance driven. Our eyes focused back on Him, our worship once again becomes presence based.

The bridge of this song is really powerful in that it gives us a revelation of the prayers of the saints rising like incense. The words are put to music around a really cool chord progression. The lyrics go like this:

"Day and night, night and day, let incense arise
Day and night, night and day, let incense arise" (2x)

Revelation 5:8   The Prayers of the Saints Rise as Incense

*When He had taken the book, the four living creatures and the twenty-four elders fell down before the Lamb, each one holding a harp and golden bowls full of **incense**, which are the **prayers** of the **saints.***

Revelation 8:4

*And the smoke of the **incense**, with the **prayers** of the **saints**, went up before God out of the angel's hand.*

We Should Still Behold the Lamb

John 1:25-27, 29 John the Baptist's declaration:
"**Behold**, the Lamb of God . . ."

> ²⁵ *They asked him (John the Baptist), "Why then are you baptizing, if you **are not** the Christ (the Messiah), nor Elijah, nor the prophet?"*
>
> ²⁶ *John answered them saying, "I baptize with water, but among you stands One whom you do not **know.**"*
>
> ²⁷ *"It is He who comes after me, the thong of whose sandal I am **not worthy** to untie."*
>
> ²⁹ *The next day he saw Jesus coming to him and said, **"Behold, the Lamb of God who** takes away the sin of the world!"*

I find that beholding the Lamb of God on a daily basis has made me a much stronger believer. Jesus as the Core of Everything has kept me focused on serving God and helping people. There are so many distractions in life anyway.

I wake up talking to the Lord, I continue the conversation throughout my day and I go to bed talking to the Lord. You don't have to be in fulltime ministry to live this as a lifestyle. You do it as an attitude of your heart and a focus of your soul.

Second, What Heaven Knows

They know Who He is, His awesome worth. They know from His appearance the justice and judgment that is coming.

What is it that Heaven knows? It is the **awesome worth** (worthiness) of the Son of God. All of Heaven recognizes His value, His goodness, His excellence and His stature and significance. They all knew Him as the Eternal One with no end.

They also know from His appearance that justice and judgment are coming. The sin and the evil that is rampant in the earth will not go on forever. The Lord is a holy God. He will not be overridden by the desires and whims of men. The day of reckoning is coming for every man and woman. God's judgment will not be delayed forever.

Revelation 1:13-18

> ¹³ *. . . I saw one like a **Son of Man** . . . .*
>
> ¹⁴ ***His head** and **His hair** were white like white wool, like snow; and **His eyes** were like a **flame of fire.***

¹⁵ ***His feet*** *were like burnished bronze, when it has been made to glow in a furnace, and **His voice** was like the sound of many waters.*

¹⁶ *In His right hand He held seven stars, and out of **His mouth** came a sharp two-edged sword; and **His face** was like the sun shining in its strength.*

¹⁷ *When I saw Him, I fell at His feet like a dead man. And He placed His right hand on me, saying, "Do not be afraid; I am the first and the last,*

¹⁸ *and the living One; and I was dead, and behold, I am **alive forevermore**, and I have the **keys of death** and of Hades."*

Here is a picture of the mighty God that you are serving. When you begin to contemplate His greatness, it helps you see into another realm. It helps you to have big faith and more adequate grace for your daily journey.

Check the description of Who He is once again:

❖ **His head** and His hair were like white wool, like snow.

> Daniel 7:9 - *His vesture was like white snow*
> *And the hair of His head like pure wool.* (NAS)

❖ **His eyes** were like a flame of fire.

> *. . . and His eyes [**flashed**] like a flame of fire* (AMP)
> *His eyes blazed like a fiery flame;* (Voice)
> *His eyes **penetrated** like flames of fire.* (TLB, Taylor.)

> Daniel 10:6 - *His face had the appearance of **lightning**,*
> *His eyes were like flaming torches.* (NAS)

❖ **His feet** were like burnished bronze, glowing in a furnace.

> Daniel 10:6 *His arms and feet like the gleam*
> *of polished bronze.* (NAS)

❖ **His voice** was like the sound of many waters.

> *His voice filled the air and sounded like a **roaring waterfall**.*
> *And His voice thundered like mighty ocean waves.* (NLT)
> *His voice was like the noise of flooding water,*
> *the **sound** of **raging waters**.* (ERV, GWD)

> Daniel 10:6 - *and the voice of His words like the*
> *voice of a multitude.* (KJV)

❖ Out of **His mouth** came a sharp two-edged sword.

. . . from His mouth darted a sharp double-edged sword.

❖ **His face** was like the sun shining in its strength.

And His face was as bright as the sun in all its brilliance. (NLT)
. . . and His face shone a brilliant light, like the blinding sun.
His glance resembled the sun when it is
shining with its full strength. (WNT)

Pour My Love On You

In the lyrics of a current worship song about Jesus, it says this,

"I know that Your eyes are like flames of fire.
I know that Your head is white as wool.
I know that Your voice sounds like waters.
Jesus, You are beautiful."

The title of this song is "Pour my love on You." It actually starts with a chorus from a Philips, Craig and Dean song. The four parts after it are spontaneous choruses that singers Matt Gilman and others created while doing a Prayer Room set.

The lyrics remind us, the more time we spend in prayer and the Word, the more the Holy Spirit reveals the Person of the Lord Jesus.

From a Lamb to a Lion, Coming Back Again

"Before He is called *a **lion;***
here He appears *as a **lamb*** *slain.*
He is a ***lion*** to conquer satan,
a ***lamb*** to **satisfy** the **justice** of God.
He appears with the marks of His sufferings upon Him,
to show that He **interceded** in heaven
in the virtue of His satisfaction."

(Matthew Henry Commentary)

All of Heaven recognizes the "power of the life of the crucified Lamb." They know Jesus as the Overcomer. He has overcome. His eternal glory and stature are on display. No one else was found "worthy" to break the seals of the scroll or look into it, but Jesus was deemed "Worthy" because He had **overcome.**

Overcame what?
Death, hell and the grave.
He overcame
the evil nature of the human race, including
pride and prejudice,
greed, self-centeredness and selfishness.

*"Stop weeping; behold, the Lion that is from the tribe of Judah, the Root of David, **has overcome** so as to open the scroll and its seven seals." Revelation 5: 5*

John 16:23-24, 33 The **"Prayer Works"** Promise
because Jesus overcame.

[23] *. . . I say to you, if you ask the Father for anything **in My name**, He will give it to you.*

[24] *. . . **ask** and **you will receive**,*
so that your joy may be made full.

[33] *"These things I have spoken to you, so that in Me you may **have peace**. In the world you have tribulation, but take courage; I have **overcome** the world."*

This is the connection between worship, prayer and music and the Lord Jesus overcoming all the things that try to keep us from it. His overcoming has made a way for us to create music that flows from consecrated hearts; music truly dedicated to the Lord.

The power of worship as it comes from born again hearts happens because He has broken every chain and set us free from our bondages. Worship flows best from hearts that are free.

This brings us to the topic of prayer. There would be no intercession if He had not overcome, the world, the flesh, the devil. We would still be a part of all of that, except Jesus' love intervened in the middle of our messy lives. We have been changed and lifted to new spiritual realms where justice is becoming a key centerpiece of how we live our lives. The power to be an intercessor directly comes from His Lordship and His authority because of everything He overcame.

We must talk more about Jesus. We must study more about Jesus. We must apprehend more about His beauty and the realm He lives in. We must know more about His being and the ultimate goodness and grace that emanates from His face and His eyes.

Third, How then does Heaven respond?

Third, how then does Heaven respond? Heaven's response is to worship the Person of the Lord Jesus in their midst. Our place is to do the same thing Heaven does, "Behold the Lamb of God, know Him and respond."

Revelation 5:4-8 Who Heaven Sees and What Heaven
Knows and How Heaven Responds

[4] *Then I began to weep greatly because **no one** was **found worthy** to open the scroll or to look into it;*

[5] *and one of the elders said to me,*
*"Stop weeping; behold, the Lion that is from the tribe of Judah, the Root of David, **has overcome***
so as to open the scroll and its seven seals."

[6] *And I saw in the middle of the throne and of the four living creatures and in the middle of the elders*
a Lamb standing, as if slain,
having seven horns and seven eyes, which are the seven Spirits of God, sent out into all the earth.

[7] *And He came and took the scroll (the book)out of the right hand of Him who sat on the throne.*

[8] *When He had taken the scroll,*
the four living creatures and
*the twenty-four elders **fell down before the Lamb**,*

*each one holding a **harp** and golden **bowls** full of incense, which are the **prayers** of the **saints** (the holy ones).*

The "Greatness and the Glory"

Being totally overwhelmed by the glory and the greatness of Jesus, the Lamb that was slain, they **fell down**. This is how Heaven responds. They recognized His awesome majesty.

31

His holiness was fully on display. This is the only proper response to hearts on fire.

It was just 'too much' glory! It was too much greatness as they beheld the Lamb of God, slain. They could no longer hold their places. Other translations say, "they fell prostrate before Him." They literally fell on their face because of the power and the glory. What a scene this must be in Heaven!!

This response cannot be interrupted because His worth commands it, Who He is even demanded it. They were expressing **adoration** and **worship** for Jesus Christ Himself. This is the power of the life of the Crucified Lamb, Who is coming back as the Lion of Judah.

Worship Full of Reverential Awe

Psalm 2:11-12

> [11] **Worship** the LORD with reverence (reverential awe) and rejoice with **trembling**. Serve the Lord with reverent awe and **worshipful fear**; rejoice and be in high spirits with trembling [lest you displease Him].

> [12] Do homage to the Son, that He not become angry, and you perish in the way, for soon shall His wrath be kindled. (NAS, AMP)

> > Kiss the Son [pay **devotion** to Him in purity],
> > (show allegiance, revere and awe the Lord).

(When) they *fell down before Him,* they gave Him not an **inferior** sort of worship, but the most **profound adoration**.

The instruments used in their adorations--
> *harps and vials (bowls or containers);*
> the harps were the instruments of praise,
> the bowls were full of incense,
> which signify *the prayers of the saints:*

Prayer and worship should always go together.

(Matthew Henry Commentary)

32

Prayer and worship should always go together. This is the sentiments of my heart exactly. For me personally, I don't ever want to do prayer that is not supported by anointed music. And I don't have to because prayer and worship are found running together throughout the Word of God.

Revelation 5:9-10

> [9] *And they sang a new song, saying,*
>
> *"**Worthy** are You to take the scroll and to break its seals;*
> *for **You were slain**, and **purchased** for God*
>
> *with **Your blood** men from every tribe and*
> *tongue and people and nation."*
>
> [10] *"You have made them to be a kingdom and*
> ***priests to our God**; and they will reign upon the earth."*

His sacrifice, death and
        resurrection **genuinely** makes Jesus

    . . . **worthy** of all affection and praise,
          (universally, before all men).

    . . . **worthy** of our life's dedication to worship,
          intercession and prayer.

Jesus is   . . . the Master Lord over all spirits.
      . . . His light in power dispels all darkness.
      . . . His great grace is superior to the works of men.
      . . . His justice triumphs over all wickedness.
      . . . and His redemption covers the fallen state of man.

Streaming in Heaven's Flow

Jesus is The Core of Everything

Worthy is the Lamb that was Slain,
He Made Us to be a Kingdom of Priests

Revelation 5:6, 9-10

I. Who is it That Heaven Sees?

A. The Person of the Lord Jesus

Jesus was a real person who walked on the earth. The very being of the Son of God was here in human form and then returned to all of His glory.

1) Jesus, the Lamb of God, slain
2) He is beautiful beyond all description
3) Heaven sees Him "ever living to make intercession"

B. Beholding Who Jesus Is

It will take dedicated, additional amounts of time to even scratch the surface to know of the revelation of Jesus.

1) He is an example of dedication and devotion, so we should be too!

2) Every believer needs to live some part of their life in dedicated times of deeper devotion to Him, to know His ways and know Him intimately.

C. You Are Worthy of It All

Revelation 4:11

*Thou art **worthy**, O Lord, to receive glory and honor and power: for Thou hast created **all** things,
and **for Thy pleasure** they are and were created.* (KJV)

1) All the saints and angels bow
2) Elders cast their crowns
3) Four living creatures cry "holy" continually

D. We Should Still Behold the Lamb

I find that beholding the Lamb of God on a daily basis has

made me a much stronger believer. Jesus as the Core of Everything has kept me focused to serve God and help people.

II. What Heaven Knows

A. The Description of Who He is

1) **His head** and His hair were like white wool, like snow
2) **His eyes** were like a flame of fire
3) **His feet** were like burnished bronze,
   glowing in a furnace
4) **His voice** was like the sound of many waters
5) Out of **His mouth** came a sharp two-edged sword
6) **His face** was like the sun shining in its strength

B. From a Lamb to a Lion, Coming Back Again

All of Heaven recognizes the
   "power of the life of the crucified Lamb."

1) Worship flows best from hearts that are free.
2) There would be no intercession if He had not
   overcome, the world, the flesh and the devil.

III. How Then Does Heaven Respond?

A. The "Greatness and the Glory"

B. Worship Full of Reverential Awe

Jesus is
   . . . the Master Lord over all spirits.
   . . . His light in power dispels all darkness.
   . . . His great grace is superior to the works of men.
   . . . His justice triumphs over all wickedness.
   . . . and His redemption covers the fallen state of man.

Again:

1) All the saints and angels bow
2) Elders cast their crowns
3) Four living creatures cry "holy" continually

The Prayers of the Saints

*The prayers of the saints
come up before God
in a cloud of incense;
no prayer, thus recommended,
was ever denied audience or acceptance.*

*"When He (Jesus) had taken the scroll;
the four living creatures
and the twenty-four elders
fell down [and worshipped,
they bowed down] before the Lamb
each one holding
a harp and golden bowls full of incense,
which are the prayers of the saints."*
Revelation 5:8

Chapter Three

The Prayers of the Saints

The Ministry of Worship and Intercession

Revelation 5:7-8

⁷ And He came [a Lamb standing, as if slain] and took the scroll [the book]; out of the right hand of Him who sat on the throne.

*⁸ When He had taken the scroll [the book]; the four living creatures and the twenty-four elders fell down [and **worshipped**, they bowed down]*

*before the Lamb each one holding a **harp** and golden **bowls** full of incense, which are the **prayers** of the **saints**.*

(MSG, ERV)

The Ministry of Worship and Intercession

This is why we pray, to release the power of God's Word. We sing and pray the Word of God in power . . . to release the desires and purposes of our Heavenly Father for the earth. We are His vessels helping to release the written judgments of God that defeat His enemies.

In Revelation chapter five, each one of the 24 elders were holding a harp in one hand and golden bowls full of incense which are the prayers of the saints [holy ones].

This is Heaven's model of worship and prayer. As we peer into Heaven, through this scripture, we see the importance of worship and the prayers of the Saints. It gives us a blueprint of how we can do sustainable worship and prayer. So we are "Streaming in Heaven's Flow!"

Revelation 5:8

*And when He had taken the book, the four beasts and the four and twenty rulers went down on their faces before the Lamb, having every one an **instrument of music**, and gold **vessels** full of perfumes, which are the prayers of the saints.* (BBE)

So what we are seeing here is the power of anointed music combined with prayer and worship. How wonderful this whole scenario is. Through our God-given singing gifts, music gifts and a sanctified heart we can begin to do that which is modeled in Heaven. Our music establishes the base and support for worship and prayer ascending before the Lord.

Holding a Harp - [kithara]-(kē-thä'-rä)

*and [they] **worshipped**, before the Lamb each one holding a **harp*** (Revelation 5:8)

Definition: a harp to which praises of God are sung in heaven.

A harp is a musical instrument with strings stretched vertically in an open, triangular frame and played by plucking with the fingers. This definition also means to persist in talking continuously, to harp at. It also means writing tediously or continuously (*on, upon* something).
[Please stop harping at me.] Rare definition: to give voice to.

Music (harping) that is touched by the Lord's anointing becomes a weapon of war in the spirit realm, against the kingdom of darkness just as God has intended.

Music helps focus the attention of those doing prayer and intercession on the Lord. In general, if the music stops during a meeting, everyone looks forward to see what is going on and what we are going to do next. Music like in photography helps us keep our focal point. It is something that helps us pay attention. We use music as a bed or foundation, to enter into the priestly ministry of prayer and worship. This is the highest usage of music.

The power of anointed music played through consecrated vessels has its own authority.

The Confirmation of the Importance of the Prayers of the Saints

Revelation 8:3-5

> [3] *Another angel came and stood at the altar, holding a golden censer; and much* **incense** *was given to him, so that he might add it (give it) to the*
> **prayers of all the saints** *[holy ones] on the golden altar which was before the throne.*

> [4] *And the smoke of the incense, with the prayers of the saints, went up before God out of the angel's hand.*

> [5] *Then the angel took the censer and filled it with the fire of the altar, and threw it to the earth; and there followed peals of thunder and sounds and flashes of lightning and an earthquake, which are the* **prayers** *of the* **saints** *[holy ones].*

All Are Praying People - Everyone has a Voice

All the saints are a praying people;
none of the children of God are born mute,
without a voice or
incapable of operating in (His) authority.
A Spirit of grace is always a
Spirit of adoption and supplication,
teaching us to cry, Abba, Father, Abba.
(Matthew Henry's commentary)

Prayer defined is our heart-felt words addressed to God. I love the above quote because everyone has a voice. We don't need special training to begin. Some of my greatest prayer times were, as I was alone with my guitar, worshipping and pouring my heart out before the Lord. In a similar way, we had group pre-service prayer that was so anointed by God's presence we didn't want to leave that time to start the regular meeting.

We have not fully modeled, as well as understated, the power of the prayers of the saints. Most of us can only make it through one or two really boring prayer meetings. This is why we never do corporate prayer with out music supporting it. Music carries it's own God-given anointing. Most of us know this and it's one of the greatest weapons in our spiritual arsenal.

Music helps us clear the many distractions we have when we attempt to do consistent prayer. His Holy Spirit helps us with our greatest challenge which is to make a willful commitment to pray more and worship more.

Psalm 32:6 *For this shall every one*
that is godly pray unto Thee.

> *For this [forgiveness] let everyone who is godly pray--*
> *pray to You in a time when You may be found; surely*
> *when the great waters [of trial] overflow, they shall not*
> *reach [the spirit in] Him.*

❖ Prayer is **petitionary**, full of words with sacred character, directed to God as sincere prayers.

❖ Prayer expresses **access** to God and tells of a personal closeness to Him.

❖ Prayer includes the **element** of pure devotion to the Lord and to His purposes. It speaks of a childlike confidence to pray to Him . . . as the heart's conversation with God.
(Matthew Henry's Commentary)

In Light of Our Covenant Rights

We stand before the only Righteous Heavenly Judge, addressing humble prayer requests to Him Who has the power to grant them. The reason that Jesus went to the Cross for our sins is many fold. But one of the top reasons is that we would have access to our Heavenly Father, access to the Throne Room and the courts of His mercy and justice.

Let's look at four distinct types of prayer concerning the prayers of the saints.

Petition - simple requests or straightforward speech and appeals

Beseech - asking earnestly; to entreat or implore (to plead)

Supplication - to ask humbly on bended knee or
                   to call upon with great desire

Intercession - pleading someone else's case on their behalf

These four types of prayer were used by everyday people of the Bible to effect change in their situations. They were living life just as we do.

They had ups. They had downs. They had good days. They had bad days. But prayer became their companion. They learned to turn to the Lord with all of their needs because they had confidence in the God who answers prayer.

Zacharias, Timothy, Solomon and Nehemiah used prayer as a tool and a weapon, that's right, prayer was like a tool in their garden and a weapon to defeat their enemies. They knew their covenant rights and prayed from this place and position. It was God's way of giving them dominion on the earth.

To Petition . . . simple requests, straightforward
                  speech and appeals.

1 Timothy 2:1

> *[A Call to Prayer] First of all, then, I urge that entreaties and prayers, **petition**s and thanksgivings, be made on behalf of all men . . .*

We should be praying, petitioning the Lord at all times according to Ephesians 6:8. This can be done in an attitude of gratefulness irregardless of our need. The Lord never grows tired of hearing our heart and voice. We really can't wear the Lord out on this.

Luke 1:13

> *But the angel said to him, "Do not be afraid, Zacharias, for your **petition** has been **heard**, and your wife Elizabeth will bear you a son, and you will give him the name John."*

The scripture records that "you have not because you ask not." Take a few moments now and then to thank the Lord for the little things He does for you. Or, take a minute to lift up a family member or a co-worker before the Lord. This is your covenant right, take advantage of it.

Beseech ... [Be - Seek] to ask earnestly;
entreat; implore (to plead).

I personally really like this word and this type of prayer. It engages the seeking heart and puts to use the power of being earnest and genuine.

Nehemiah 1:5

> I said, "I **beseech** You, O Lord God of heaven, the great and awesome God, who **preserves** the covenant and loving-kindness for those who love Him and keep His commandments."

It's to our advantage, as we beseech the Lord, to use the Word of God as we pray, because His Word is never going to pass away. We must keep sight of the fact that we are speaking to our great and awesome God, who preserves the covenant and ask Him to grant our prayers. There is a place of "pleading your case" before the Lord. The word "plead" is full of so much intensity. It helps us understand the true meaning of beseeching the Lord prayerfully.

Nehemiah 1:11

> O Lord, I **beseech** You, may Your ear be attentive to the prayer of Your servant and the prayer of Your servants who delight to **revere Your name**, and make Your servant successful today and grant him compassion before this man (the Persian king).

Supplication ... to ask humbly on bended knee, (a kind of submission) to call upon with great desire, to entreat, earnest prayer in worship.

2Chronicles 6:19, 21   Solomon's Prayer
Dedicating the Temple

> [19] Yet have regard to the prayer of Your servant and to his **supplication**, O Lord my God, to listen to the **cry** and to the **prayer** which Your servant prays before You;

> [21] Listen to the **supplication**s of Your servant and of Your people Israel when they pray toward this place; hear from Your dwelling place, from heaven; hear and forgive.

I love how Solomon exposes his heart in front of the Lord and all the Hebrew people at the dedication of the House of the Lord. This was Solomon's place. He was a powerful governor and yet not so great in his own eyes; because he humbled his heart and entered into the attitude of being a supplicant.

Solomon was Petitioning God and Doing Supplication

2Chronicles 6:34-35, 37 and 39

> [34] *When Your people go out to battle against their enemies . . . and they **pray to You** toward this city which You have chosen and the house which I have built for Your name,*

> [35] *then hear from heaven their prayer and their **supplication**, and maintain their cause.*

> [37] *If they take thought in the land where they are taken captive, and repent and make **supplication** to You in the land of their captivity, saying, 'We have sinned, we have committed iniquity and have acted wickedly';*

> [39] *then hear from heaven, from Your dwelling place, their prayer and **supplication**s, and maintain their cause and forgive Your people who have sinned against You.*

One of the synonyms for "supplication" is to "appeal." We are appealing to the God who is infinite in power and is never overwhelmed by the darkness. So it's with a deep humility and a sincere heart that we supplicate. Don't be turned off by this word. I imagine this is a new concept for many concerning prayer. But, as we enter in and pray, the Holy Spirit helps us know that our supplications are being heard and recorded in Heaven.

Intercession . . . the act of interceding;
                            mediation [intervention],
                            pleading or prayer on behalf of others.

Romans 8:34

> *Who is He who condemns? It is Christ who died, and furthermore is also risen, who is even at the right hand of God, who also makes **intercession** for us.*

43

Intercession is the action of mediating - to go between or stand in between. This is where we intervene in the affairs of God and men. We can make an argument to win the case and settle the dispute with His holy justice.

Isn't this a wonderful thing that we partner with God in the power of His Holy Spirit and pray at this level? Further, the definition means to make up the hedge, stand in the gap. This is where warfare becomes a real part of prayer.

Prayer and intercession
crush the evil and
establish God's justice
on the earth and
binds up the activities
of the kingdom of darkness.

We can literally stand in prayer for others and help them fight their battle. It is a place of honor. Jesus does it for us and gives us the place and the right to do it for others.

When We Don't Know What to Pray

As we begin to look at Romans eight, think about this! First, when we don't know what to pray, the Holy Spirit, Himself, makes intercession for us.

This is one of the greatest blessings for a New Testament believer. How many times in our lives have we not known what to pray? This is such a help for everyone's prayer life.

Romans 8:26, 27

> [26] *Likewise the Spirit also helps in our weaknesses.*
> *For we do not know what we should pray for as we ought,*
> *but the Spirit Himself*
> > *makes **intercession** for us*
> *with groanings which cannot be uttered.*
>
> [27] *Now He who searches the hearts knows what the mind of the Spirit is, because He makes **intercession** for the saints according to the will of God.* (NKJV)

The Holy Spirit Helps Us in Our Weaknesses

Second: there's a great benefit as we pray and intercede, the Holy Spirit helps us in our weaknesses. We are built for worship. When someone meets the Lord, their heart is tuned in to Jesus' wave lengths. They are changed.

We are built for godly music. The Lord put it in our spirit and soul that music would affect us to the very core of our being. So we play and sing on for the abundance of God's glory.

We are built for prayer too. The Holy Spirit has a special mission in our lives, that is, to help us be consistent in prayer and worship. Whatever our **weakness** is in terms of lacking words, stick-to-itiveness and obedience concerning our prayer life, the Holy Spirit helps us with all of them.

Our Prayers are Incense Rising, Filling the Golden Bowls

Revelation 8:3-4

> [3] *Another angel came and stood at the altar, holding a golden censer; and **much incense** was given to him, so that he might add it (give it) to the **prayers of all the saints** [holy ones] on the golden altar which was before the throne.*

> [4] *And the smoke of the incense, with the **prayers** of the **saints**, went up before God out of the angel's hand.*

What place and honor is this to offer prayers that become incense in the hands of God? What a special place before the Lord, on bended knee; where Spirit-empowered believers start releasing words filled with the judgments written and measured out by the Lord Himself!

The weightiness and power of the prayers of the saints in this mode is massive in changing the spiritual atmosphere. So then, what has God wrought out of consecrated hearts, fixed on Him, willingly, and sacrificially praying His purposes? There is something very, very powerful about God's people praying at higher levels.

Here's the picture:

Musicians are playing and music is flowing where the

river of His presence starts being released.

Singers are singing and worship is rising at the sound of voices in holy array.

Leaders are praying, intercession expanding using the Word of God to prevail over the darkness.

Prayer warfare is working as it joins the sound of Heaven; effective prayers have made their marks.

This is what the Prayer Room looks like to me, corporate prayer with powerful music. I've seen the power of God released in intercession that rides on dynamic music and the depths of Spirit-touched worship and **it is unstoppable**. Do you get the picture?

The Great Effects of Our Worship and Prayers

Here's a tremendous personal story about the worship and prayers of the saints. I was doing a night of worship and intercession at a church in North Carolina.

I distinctly remember this because the ceiling of the church looked like the upside down version of Noah's Ark. It had big wooden timbers arching across the ceiling [like a vaulted ceiling]. About 30 minutes into this night, I was leading from the piano and had my eyes closed during worship. We were deep into Heaven's Flow and almost all the people were totally engaged.

I felt the Lord speak to me, "Look out at the people." I heard this in my heart but I kept playing and singing but still had not opened my eyes. Again I heard the Lord say, "Look out at the people." As I opened my eyes and looked at the congregation, light was coming out of everyone's mouth, some worshipping, and some praying. It was an awesome sight to behold. Everything was getting more intense in the room.

I looked up at the ceiling of the church and it had become translucent, semi-clear so that I could see through to the outside. As I was looking up, a rectangular, clear glass box came down through the ceiling. Within a matter of minutes all the lights began moving toward that glass box. They all arrived at the same time.

And when they did, I heard "whoosh" and all the lights turned in a circle and shot out of the top of this glass box through the ceiling like a giant laser beam. Earlier, as I was looking through the ceiling, I could see this dark canopy of clouds filled with demonic activity.

When this laser beam hit that dark cloud, it shot through it and the clouds began to roll backwards. It was like the reverse of a nuclear bomb. It was rolling outward in a 360 degree circle that created a large hole where I saw things moving very fast up and down. All the while, people were still worshipping, they were still praying.

I asked the Lord, what are these things moving so quickly up and down through the cloud of darkness? It was like hitting slow motion on your DVD player. The picture slowed down and I saw that the things were angels; angels descending, angels ascending. They were carrying and delivering the messages of God. They were the "ministers who were like flames of fire."

Hebrews 1:7 *And of the angels He says, "WHO MAKES HIS ANGELS WINDS, AND HIS MINISTERS A FLAME OF FIRE."*

The Importance of People's Pure Worship and Prayers

I would put this experience in the category of a spiritual vision where the Lord was showing me the importance of people's pure worship and prayers. They have a giant effect against the kingdom of darkness.

I really believe in the prayers of the saints. I believe in the power of worship as it streams to almighty God. We may only understand a small portion of what really takes place in the second heavens when we are praying and worshipping.

This is What We're Shooting For

Prayer **lifestyle**: It's a life that has developed worship and prayer both as the way of deep devotion to Jesus but also as a tool and a weapon against God's enemies.

Prayer **furnace**: This is where a certain flame of the Lord is ignited through significant prayer daily. It especially comes into play during corporate prayer in a prayer room.

The prayers of the saints
come up before God
in a cloud of incense;
no prayer, thus recommended,
was ever denied audience or acceptance.

The Sacred Doings of the Priest

As we will discuss in Chapter Five, the priestly ministry of prayer and worship is sometimes defined as "the sacred doings" of the priests. It's described by a peculiar word called "**sacerdotal**." It is defining the activities and functions of the priest doing ministry before the Lord.

The reason I point this out is that every day believers doing prayer and worship ministry are involved in the sacred doings as a priest.

Sacerdotal - [sak' r dōt ' l] pertaining to priests, or the priesthood, [priestly], as sacerdotal dignity, sacerdotal functions or garments, sacerdotal character   (Noah Webster 1828 Dictionary)

As we can see, this word defines part of the ministry we are called to as New Testament priests. We are a kingdom of priests. We are part of the Royal Priesthood (IPeter 2:9).

As we do more prayer and worship, there is an unveiling that takes place in our hearts. We start seeing the different aspects of the priestly office where we are busy with the "sacred doings."

Psalm 141:1-3 An Evening Prayer for
Sanctification and Protection

[1] *O LORD, I call upon You; hasten to me! Give ear to my voice when I call to You!*

[2] *May **my prayer** be counted (set forth)*
                                        as incense before You;
The lifting up of my hands as the evening offering. (NAS, AMP)

48

³ *Set a guard, O LORD, over my mouth; keep watch over the door of my lips.*

Other translations of verse two say it this way:

² *Treat my prayer as **sweet incense rising** . . .* (MSG)

² *Lord, accept my prayer. Let it be like a gift of **burning incense**. Let it be like the evening sacrifice.* (ERV)

The Intercession of Christ

What ministry is the Resurrected Christ currently doing? Most people do not know the answer to this question. It is openly revealed in Hebrews chapter seven. He ever lives to make intercession for us. How very personal of the Lord. He was aware of the covering that we would need and now He provides it.

Hebrews 7: 24-26

²⁵ *Therefore He is able also to save forever those who draw near to God through Him, since He always lives **to make intercession** for them.* (NAS)

²⁵ *Therefore He is able also to save to the uttermost (completely, perfectly, finally, and for all time and eternity) those who come to God through Him,*

*since **He is always living***

***to make petition to God and intercede** with Him and intervene for them.* (AMP)

²⁴ *But, He, by reason of His remaining age-abidingly, un-transmissible, holds, the priesthood.*

²⁵ *Whence He is able, even to be saving unto the very end, them who approach, through Him, unto God; since He evermore lives to be **interceding in their behalf**.*

²⁶ *For, such a High-Priest as this, for us, was even-suited: Loving... noble... undefiled... set apart from sinners... and become higher than the heavens.* (REB)

I want to do the ministry that Jesus is currently doing. I want to be involved in the deep love heart that Jesus has for all the saints and sinners. Yes there are people who will tell you no. But I am not taking no for an answer. There are people who will say "that's too much work and responsibility. I like better my life of comfort and ease." I will disregard that comment as well.

Since He is always living to make petitions to God, to intercede for us, it's only right that I give a part of my life to do the same for others. Think of the importance of prayer and intercession in light of the Lord's great sacrifice, His teaching and the commission He left us to fulfill.

Angels Released by God's because
The Saints were Praying!

Acts 12:6-16

> ⁶ On the very night when Herod was about to bring him forward, Peter was sleeping between two soldiers, bound with two chains, and guards in front of the door were watching over the prison.

> ⁷ And behold, **an angel of the Lord** suddenly appeared and **a light shone** in the cell; and he struck Peter's side and woke him up, saying,
> "Get up quickly." And his chains fell off his hands.

> ⁸ The angel said to him, "Gird yourself and put on your sandals." And he did so. And he said to him, "Wrap your cloak around you and follow me."

> ⁹ And he went out and continued to follow, and he did not know that what was being done by the angel **was real**, but thought he was seeing a **vision**.

> ¹⁰ When they had passed the first and second guard, they came to the iron gate that leads into the city, which **opened for them by itself**; and they went out and went along one street, and immediately the angel departed from him.

> ¹¹ When Peter **came to himself**, he said, "Now I know for sure that the Lord has sent forth His angel and **rescued me from the hand of Herod** and from all that the Jewish people were expecting."

> ¹² And when he realized this, he went to the house of Mary, the mother of John who was also called Mark, where many were gathered together and **(they) were praying.**
> The house was packed with praying friends. (MSG)

¹³ *When he knocked at the door of the gate, a servant-girl named Rhoda came to answer.*

¹⁴ *When she recognized Peter's voice, because of her joy she did not open the gate, but ran in and announced that Peter was standing in front of the gate.*

¹⁵ *They said to her, "You are out of your mind!" But she kept insisting that it was so. They kept saying, "It is his angel."*

¹⁶ *But Peter continued knocking; and when they had opened the door, they saw him and were amazed.*

There shouldn't be any doubt in anyone's mind that praying can produce supernatural results. These scriptures show the significant results of what happens when **"the prayers of the saints"** go forth.

An old time preacher years ago said as he was speaking "why pray when you can worry?" Of course, he was being comical and facetious. He was preaching on the power of prayer and how so many people find it unimportant.

This twelfth chapter of the book of Acts is so heartening isn't it? God still does miracles and He is still listening for every one of your prayers. Whether your prayer times are in a corporate setting like the Prayer Room or a personal time of devotion in your home or car . . . pray more, worship more . . . and when you're finished, pray more and worship more.

The Prayers of the Saints

The Ministry of Worship and Intercession

Revelation 5:7-8 ... *the four living creatures and the twenty-four elders fell down,* **worshipped***, they bowed down.*

I. The Ministry of Worship and Intercession

This is why we pray, to release the power of God's Word.

A. We Sing and Pray the Word of God in Power to release God's desires and purposes: to help Him release the written judgments that defeat His enemies.

B. This is Heaven's Model of Worship and Prayer

Harps in one hand representing music and worship, golden **bowl**s full of incense which are the prayers of the saints. This speaks of the ministry of worship and intercession as they are joined together.

C. Revelation 5:8 - Gives Us a Blueprint, a Heavenly Model

We can do sustainable worship and prayer like this "Streaming in Heaven's Flow!" Worship, prayer, music.

II. The Importance of the Prayers of the Saints

A. All Are Praying People - Everyone has a Voice

All the saints are a praying people; none of the children of God are born mute, without a voice or incapable of operating in (His) authority.

B. This is why we never do corporate prayer without music supporting it. Music carries it's own God-given anointing.

Music is one of the greatest weapons in our spiritual arsenal. Music helps us clear the many distractions we have when we attempt to do consistent prayer.

C. In Light of Our Covenant Rights

Zacharias, Timothy, Solomon and Nehemiah used prayer like a tool in their garden and a weapon to defeat their enemies.

1) **Petition** - simple requests with straightforward speech and appeals.

   I Timothy 2:1 - *I urge that entreaties, prayers, **petitions** and thanksgivings, be made on behalf of all men . . .*

2) **Beseech** - Be - Seek] asking earnestly; entreat or implore (to plead).

   We keep "be seeking" the Lord. Our great and awesome God, who preserves the covenant, granting our prayers.

3) **Supplication** - to ask humbly on bended knee or to call upon with great desire.

   Infinite in power, the Lord is never overwhelmed by the darkness. So it's with a humble heart that we supplicate.

4) **Intercession** - mediation, intervention, pleading, praying on behalf of others, interceding.

   We can stand in prayer for others and help them fight their battle. It is a place of honor. Jesus does it for us and gives us the place and the right to do it for others.

III. When We Don't Know What to Pray

A. The Holy Spirit Helps Us in Our Weaknesses

Romans 8 : 26, 27 - *For we do not know what we should pray for as we ought, but the Spirit Himself makes **intercession** for us*

IV. Our Prayers are Incense Rising

Psalm 141 : 1 - 2   [1] *O LORD, I call upon You; hasten to me! Give ear to my voice when I call to You!*

[2] *Treat my prayer as sweet incense rising . . .* (MSG)

[2] *Lord, accept my prayer. Let it be like a gift of burning incense. Let it be like the evening sacrifice.*   (ERV)

V. The Intercession of Christ - Hebrews 7:25

What ministry is the Resurrected Christ currently doing?
He ever lives to make intercession for us.
How very personal of the Lord. He was aware of the covering that we would need and now He provides it.
. . . since He ever lives to be **interceding on their behalf**.

Because of Love

The reason that we worship is because of Love.
The reason that we pray is because of Love.
We love Him because He first loved us.

The power to sustain a lifestyle of
worship and prayer comes from
the baseline of true love.

I heard this statement many years ago,
"lovers most always outwork workers
because the motivation of their heart
is love and not money.
Workers rarely outwork lovers."

Chapter Four

Because of Love

Love, Intimacy and Encountering God

Jeremiah 31:3

> *The LORD appeared to him from afar, saying,*
>   *"I have loved you with an **everlasting love**;*
>   *Therefore I have drawn you with lovingkindness."*
>
> *(The Lord says,) "I love you people with a love that continues*
> ***forever**. That is why I have continued showing you*
> *kindness."* (ERV)

The reason that we worship is because of Love. The reason that we pray is because of Love. We love Him because He first loved us. The power to sustain a lifestyle of worship and prayer comes from the baseline of true love.

I heard this statement many years ago, "that lovers will always outwork workers because the motivation of their heart is love and not money. Workers rarely outwork lovers."

I want you to pray at the highest levels. I want you to do worship and intercession and terrorize the kingdom of darkness. But you must first ask the Lord for the genuine revelation of the magnitude of His love toward you.

I use the word magnitude because I am thinking of my lessons from science on star magnitudes. The understanding of a stars brightness or mass is simply overwhelming. When you compare a light bulb in the lamp in your living room to the brightness of the noon day sun, it is hard to grasp because of the huge difference between the two.

It's much the same with God's love. The amount of love that He has towards you can really only be understood over a period of years. Thank God that this revelation is portioned out little by little helping us understand the gravity of His love. His drawing power, His ability to cover you along with the great plan and destiny is now unfolding in your life.

It Is Because of Love

It is because of love. Love is the true motivation of why people get married; why people have best friends; why we have babies; why people care for strangers, orphans and widows; why we cry at the loss of a loved one. It is because of love.

It's because of love; we all should learn how to sit and adore the Lord. Love helps us learn how to sit quietly and meditate on the Word of God. The call to work in prayer and intercession has to be preceded by our love for God and our love for people.

Jeremiah 31:3

*The LORD appeared to him from afar, saying, "I have loved you with an everlasting **love**; Therefore I have drawn you with lovingkindness."*

The Lord appeared from of old to me [Israel], saying, Yes, I have loved you with an everlasting love; therefore with loving-kindness have I drawn you and continued My faithfulness to you. (AMP)

From a distance ADONAI appeared to me, [saying,] "I love you with an everlasting love; this is why in My grace I draw you to Me." (CJB)

Then our heart responds,
"Because of Your love Lord,
I can be a lover, a friend and an intercessor
to release my love back to You."

"Streaming in Heaven's Flow," using worship, intercession and music as weapons is vitally important. But we should do it and enter into it because of a greater understanding of His love for us.

Mothers are a perfect example of unconditional love. The crying baby at 3:00 o'clock in the morning interrupting her deepest sleep is not a fun job. But because of love, she rises to care for and nurse her baby.

People who have adopted children in the United States or from other countries, are not doing so for an additional tax deduction on their taxes. They are adopting a baby or a child that has no biological association with them at all. They pay $30,000 to $50,000 to give this child their name and it is all **because of love.**

This is Our Baseline

This is our starting line. This is our baseline. We don't pray and do worship because we are workers, we do these things because of the unfolding revelation of the power of knowing God intimately. The communion of the Holy Spirit has much to do with intimacy. All things were created for His pleasure.

Years ago, at a youth conference in Arkansas, I was with a team of very powerful leaders. After two and half days of meetings in the presence of the Lord and many changed lives, we were tearing down the sound system and carrying it to the waiting van.

This young worship leader, as we were loading a speaker into the van, said, "Yeah isn't it awesome, all things were created for His pleasure. Kent, your voice was created for His pleasure. You're hands that play the guitar were created for His pleasure. Your whole life and your heart were created for His pleasure."

Revelation 4:11

> *Thou art worthy, O Lord, to receive glory honor and power: for thou hast created all things, and **for Thy pleasure** they are and were created.* (KJV)

The Greek word for pleasure is: theléma- (the'-lā-mä) - meaning the purpose of God to bless mankind through Christ. It is our Heavenly Father's choice, His desire and for His pleasure that He made us for love, for friends and a family.

> *". . . for you created all things, and because of your desire they existed, and were created."* (WEB) (Revelation 4:11)

All Things were Created for His Pleasure, Especially YOU!

This conversation changed my life forever. It really wrecked my life for two or three weeks. I kept thinking, "I am not playing my music just for people, I play my music unto the Lord because of love. I keep singing even when I am tired because of love." Through the 39 years of ministry, I have said that I would not ever work this hard for any man on the earth. But I would for Jesus because of love. In the end, He is worthy of it all. So by now as you are reading this chapter, hopefully you are deeply moved and have been captivated because of love.

Philippians 2:13

> . . . for it is God who is at work in you,
> both to will and to work for
> **His good pleasure** [and satisfaction and delight]. (NAS, AMP)

Re-Opening Our Hearts to the Strength of Love

It is hard for people to return to doing things because of love. Most of us have had so many relationships ruined that were not covered by love, we gave up. We have been abused, we have been mistreated, we have been lied to, we've been made fun of and it is not because of love. It was because of meanness, jealousy and sometimes straight up hatred.

God's love translated onto
the human plane is like the ocean,
wave after wave,
never stopping,
never having to restart itself again.

1 John 4:19

> We love, because **He first** loved us.

This is our time to begin our study of love again. Regardless of our age, regardless of the time of our life, love released bears great fruit. This was hard for me because by the time I was a teenager, I had built up so many defense mechanisms.

I had walls up against those who were trying to love me. I found it hard to separate between those who said they loved me, but actually had ulterior motives, and their own need to use me for their benefit; and those who really did love me and wanted to be true friends, sharing the things of our hearts and minds.

So fast forward into my relationship with God, fast forward into the time when I got married. It took me a few years honestly to understand that the Lord had my best interest at heart. The same is true of my wife, Carla. It was hard to believe that someone would actually love me unconditionally and make so few demands on my life otherwise.

To the point, I worshipped Jesus because I knew He had saved my scrawny, messed up life. My worship life began before I really understood the depths of His love for me. But as I continued to grow in Christ in worship, in prayer and even in my music, His love for me unfolded before my eyes.

It was the same with my marriage. I married Carla because of our shared love together. (She was a "super lover" of Jesus but also really beautiful too!) But my understanding of the depths of true love grew tremendously in the first three years we were married.

There is no room in love for fear.
*Well-formed love **banishes** fear.*
Since fear is crippling, a fearful life-
fear of death, fear of judgment-
is one not yet fully formed in love.
(I John 4:18 MSG)

There is No Fear in the Perfect Love of God

Fear is an evil taskmaster. There are so many people that don't live out the fullness of their lives because of fear. Fear produces lack of confidence, insecurity, nightmares, a certain withdrawal from reality.

Whereas love produces strength, hope, faith, joy, and an ongoing endurance. Perfect love casts out, annihilates, and makes fear go away.

1 John 4:16-19

> [16] *We have come to know and have believed*
>   *the **love** which God has for us.*
> *God is **love**, and the one who abides in love abides in God,*
> *and God abides in him.*
>
> [17] *By this, love is perfected with us, so that we may have*
> *confidence in the day of judgment; because as He is, so also*
> *are we in this world.*
>
> [18] *There is **no fear** in love;*
> *but **perfect love** casts out fear,*
>
>> *because God's perfect love drives out fear.* (NCV)
>>
>> *because fear has torment [in it],*
>>   *it involves judgment*
>> *and the one who fears is not perfected in love.*
>>
>> *has not reached the full **maturity** of love*
>> *[is not yet grown into love's complete perfection].*
>>   (AMP, KJV, NLT)
>
> [19] *We love, because He first loved us.* (NAS)

The Word of God helps us with the deeper revelation of why He loves us, why we can return love to Him freely and unconditionally and not be afraid. Let us start again, because of love, to open our hearts, to flow in worship . . . to engage in prayer . . . to read His Word and allow the cleansing that it brings. God is love. The one who abides in love abides in God. There is **no fear** in love; but perfect love casts out (all) fear.

Learning the Deeper Realm of Intimacy

John 1:18

> *No one has ever seen God. But His only Son, who is Himself God,*
> *is near to the Father's heart; He has told us about Him.* (NLT)
>
> *No man has ever seen God at any time;*
> *the only unique Son . . . Who is in the bosom*
>
> *[in the **intimate** presence] of the Father . . .* (AMP)

Intimacy is the true driver for the motivation for "Streaming in Heaven's Flow." For a life to be given fully to worship, prayer and music, there has to be a greater understanding of intimacy with God and His desire to be with us. Otherwise, we approach the doing of spiritual things as workers and not lovers.

The Amplified Bible's version of John 1:18 (on the previous page) is very enlightening. The intimacy between God the Father and God the Son is clearly defined. If we follow the point all the way through, this is the **intimacy factor** that can carry through to our lives before the Lord. Very few people will ever sustain long-term prayer and intercession without the grasp of the power of this intimacy.

We are privileged to be a part of what the Father has with the Son, and the Son has with the Father. Intimacy with God helps us walk a powerful, constant Christian life.

Love with no fear and open intimacy are major connections to the heart of God. And from the power of His presence love exudes in both directions. Many people haven't received the message of intimacy and love because they have never seen it modeled. Intimacy in the realm of prayer and worship is a great facilitator (helper).

John 15:5

> *"I am the Vine, you are the branches. When you're joined with Me and I with you, the relation **intimate** and organic, the harvest is sure to be abundant. Separated, you can't produce a thing."* (MSG)

2Corinthians 13:14

> *The amazing grace of the Master, Jesus Christ, the extravagant love of God, the **intimate friendship** of the Holy Spirit, be with all of you.* (MSG)

Our Bridal Identity

2Corinthians 11:2   The Bride of Christ
                          [from Paul to the Corinthian Believers]

> *I feel a divine jealousy for you, for I betrothed you to **Christ** to present you as a pure **bride** to her one husband.* (RSV)
>> [This verse clarifies and establishes
>>   the phrase "the Bride of Christ."]

61

When you pair the knowledge of intimacy with the Body of Christ's Bridal identity, it's a holy combination. Jesus said, "I am coming back again." The Bridegroom is coming for His Bride. "I am coming to marry You!" It is a known fact, when a woman becomes engaged, they do everything in their power to get ready and to make sure their wedding day is perfect.

It would be so embarrassing to do anything other than be totally prepared. Now transfer the importance of the Body of Christ as a Bride being ready, having prepared for her Bridegroom. There is so much eternal value on the spiritual realm compared to the natural plane.

It seems to me that the teaching of the Bride and the Bridegroom concerning the Body of Christ and the Lord Jesus has been greatly overlooked and mostly under taught.

So today, most believers are missing this essential truth which weighs intently on living a worship prayer-filled lifestyle. If we don't get certain elemental truths, we are deficient in knowledge on how to function at higher levels.

Revelation 22:17

> The **Spirit** and the **Bride** say, "Come." And let the one who hears say, "Come." And let the one who is thirsty come; let the one who wishes take the water of life without cost.

> The [Holy] Spirit and the **bride**
> (the church, the true Christians) say, Come! (AMP)

Revelation 19:7 **His bride** prepared herself, made herself ready.

> Let us rejoice and shout for joy [exulting and triumphant]!
> Let us celebrate and give to Him the glory and the honor,
> for the marriage of the Lamb [at last] has come,
> and **His bride** has prepared herself, made herself ready.
> (AMP, NAS)

I believe this great revelation of our Bridal Identity and intimacy helps us fulfill our priestly ministry of prayer and worship. This leads to taking advantage of the possibilities of a full worship life. To avoid a luke-warm spiritual walk before the Lord, the knowledge of our Bridal Identity must have a place of importance in our lives.

Encounters with Jesus

My good friend Kirk Bennett came to my church and the Destiny Prayer Room in February of 2008. He was a great help in the development of the Prayer Room and how to release people in the truths of Streaming in Heaven's Flow with worship and prayer.

Kirk kept using this phrase as he was teaching, "We must help people encounter God more. Helping people encounter God benefits us all in terms of growing a deeper spiritual life." Quite frankly, I did not like the term "encounter." It seemed foreign to me and fairly impersonal.

I realized after about two months of resisting this phrase, "encountering God," that it really sums up the need for everyday believers to pray more and worship more. As leaders in the Prayer Room, we needed terminology and language that would help people understand their need to know the Lord better. So I began using it myself.

Encounter - to come upon face-to-face; to come upon or experience especially unexpectedly; to meet with personally; to cross paths with and experience the qualities of their life.

Here are some of the greatest "Encountering God" moments in the New Testament. I believe we will see similar events as we deepen our prayer and worship lives in His presence.

A Forgiveness Encounter - The Woman Taken in Adultery

John 8:3-11

> [3] *And the scribes and Pharisees brought unto Him a woman taken in adultery; and when they had set her in the midst,*

⁴ They say unto Him, Master, this woman was taken in adultery, in the very act.

⁵ Now Moses in the law commanded us, that such should be stoned: but what do You say? ⁶ This they said, tempting Him, that they might have something of which to accuse Him.

But Jesus stooped down, and with His finger wrote on the ground, as though He heard them not.

⁷ So when they continued asking Him, He lifted up Himself, and said unto them, he that is without sin among you, let him first cast a stone at her.

⁸ And again He stooped down, and wrote on the ground.

⁹ And they which heard it,
   *being **convicted** by their own **conscience**,*
went out one by one, beginning at the oldest,
   even unto the last:
and Jesus was left alone,
   and the woman standing in the midst.

¹⁰ When Jesus had lifted up Himself,
   and saw none but the woman,
He said unto her, Woman, where are your accusers?
   Has no man condemned thee?

¹¹ She said, No one, Lord. And Jesus said unto her, Neither do I condemn you: go, and sin no more. (KJV, NKJV)

How I love this story. Instead of Jesus siding with the Pharisees, according to all the legalities of the law, He chose love. He chose forgiveness. Verse six tells us that He bent down and wrote something in the dirt. He actually did it two different times (see verse 8). Now what would He have been writing with His finger in the dirt?

I believe it's plausible that Jesus began writing in the dust the sins of all the men, the same men that had thrown this woman at Jesus' feet. It is possible they had visited prostitutes and kept their sin secret. It is possible that one or two of them could have slept with the woman at Jesus' feet.

Ephesians 2:3-7 Because of His Great Love

³ Among them (sons of disobedience) we too all formerly lived in the lusts of our flesh, indulging the desires of the flesh and the mind, and were by nature children of wrath, even as the rest.

⁴ *But God, being* **rich** *in* **mercy***, because of* **His great love** *with which He loved us.*

When He was finished writing in the dirt, He said, "Woman where are your accusers?" She meekly said, "They are all gone." He forgave her and said, "Go your way and sin no more."

As we spend additional hours in worship and intercession, we will have multiple face-to-face encounters with the Lord. I am looking forward to my next forgiveness encounter.

Genuine encounters with God are one of our only hopes for a great awakening and turning our Nation back to God.

A Healing Encounter - Ten Lepers Encounter Jesus

Luke 17:12-19

¹² *And as He entered into a certain village, there met Him ten men that were lepers, which stood afar off:*
¹³ *And they lifted up their voices, and said, Jesus, Master, have mercy on us.*
¹⁴ *And when He saw them, He said unto them, Go show yourselves unto the priests. And it came to pass, that, as they went, they were cleansed.*

¹⁵ *And one of them, when he saw that he was healed, turned back, and with a loud voice glorified God,*
¹⁶ *And fell down on his face at His feet, giving Him thanks: and he was a Samaritan.*
¹⁷ *And Jesus answering said, Were there not ten cleansed? But where are the nine?*
¹⁸ *There are not found that returned to give glory to God, save this stranger.*
¹⁹ *And He said unto him, arise, go thy way:*
               thy faith hath made thee whole. (KJV)

Here is Jesus preparing to release the healing of Heaven into those whose skin was literally falling off. They were outcasts, they were unclean, and they were full of disease. Jesus is the Healer. But He also knew the law of Moses, so He told them in faith, "Go show yourselves to the priest." He understood this was appropriate for the completion of their healing. He fully knew that as they turned from Him, they would be cleansed. And so it was.

But only one returned. Only one out of ten returned. How rude. How disrespectful to Jesus personally! These verses record that this leper that He called "the stranger" was not only healed, he was completely made whole.

This kind of healing is found when we encounter God. We have seen people while they are interceding and warring in the Spirit totally healed while they were praying. They didn't even realize it until they were finished. We have had people sitting in the Prayer Room not doing much of anything in the presence of the Lord totally healed.

Jesus is the healing ointment for every sickness and disease. Jeremiah, the prophet, asked the question, "Is there no Balm in Gilead?"

Jeremiah 8:22

> Is there no **balm** in **Gilead**? Is there no physician there? Why then has not the health of the daughter of my people been restored?
>
> [Because Zion no longer enjoyed the presence of the Great Physician!] (AMP)
>
> Are there no **healing ointments** in Gilead? Isn't there a doctor in the house? So why can't something be done to heal and save my dear, dear people? (MSG)

The reason for Jeremiah's question is that he knew that if there is no balm (ointment) left in Gilead, then there would be no healing available in the land. Most of all oils and spices used for anointing and healing were grown in Ramoth in the Gilead region.

The region of Gilead was known for the fertileness of its soil. They also possessed the pure seed stock for all their bushes and trees which produced oils and resins. They also had adequate rain fall and long growing seasons.

Jesus knew the history of the Hebrew people and was schooled in the facts of healing oils and ointments. Greater yet, He knew HE was the Balm of Gilead.

A Revelation and Light Encounter –

John on the Isle of Patmos

Revelation 1:1-3

> [1] *The **Revelation** of Jesus Christ, which God gave Him to show to His bond-servants, the things which must soon take place; and He sent and communicated it by His angel to His bond-servant John.*
>
> [2] *Who testified to the word of God and to the testimony of Jesus Christ, even to **all** that he **saw**.*
>
> [3] *Blessed is he who reads and those who hear the words of the prophecy, heed the things which are written in it; for the time is near.*

There is such a light transmitted to your spirit when you are praying and worshipping. I realized a number of years ago that Destiny Church's staff and pastors gained new revelation from the time they spent being in the Prayer Room.

Whether you are involved in personal devotion in your home or car, or you engage in corporate prayer and worship in a public setting, new light and revelation are sure to come to your heart.

Some actually feel that the book of Revelation and what happened to John the Apostle, was a one time event only and never to be paralleled again.

But it is easy to see, even though it is quite overwhelming, that this **God-encounter**, produced huge revelation as the Light of Heaven was pouring into John's soul and spirit.

The Lord has an ongoing personal invitation to each one of us every day to come and be with Him. We may say no and bypass this amazing opportunity or we may say yes and be totally distracted even though we are trying to engage in prayer.

The point is, God-encounters produce tremendous effects in our spiritual growth.

The Eternal Encounter - The Cross

John 19:30   The greatest love words ever spoken:

. . . He said, **"It is finished!"**
> And He bowed His head and gave up His spirit.

Jesus was God but He laid aside all of His glory to put on an earth suit, a human body made from clay, just like us. I wonder if the angels stood confounded as the knowledge in Heaven became known that Jesus was going to earth.

Jesus encountered God the Father, encountered demonic spirits and encountered the full force of our sins and the hatred of thousands of human beings. Because of love. Because of such great love. The greatest thing that held Him to the Cross was LOVE. This experience was the ultimate time and eternity encounter.

God's plan is that love would abound
on the earth forever.
Love is more than
just a key thread in the tapestry
of the salvation story.
It is the main purpose
in God's storyline.

1Corinthians 13:13

> *Now abide faith, hope, love, these three;*
> > *but the greatest of these is love.*

> *. . . love--true affection for God and man, growing out of God's love for and in us], these three; but the greatest of these is love.* (AMP)

*So these three things **continue forever**: faith, hope, and love.
And the greatest of these is love.* (NCV)

*But for right now, until that completeness, we have three things
to do to lead us toward that consummation:*

***Trust** steadily in God, **hope** unswervingly, **love** extravagantly.
And the best of the three is love.* (MSG)

Love: The Core Message of the Kingdom

Love is the main purpose in God's storyline that He communicated to Abraham, Moses, David, and all the prophets. It is the fulfillment of the law and prophets.

Love is the greatest virtue, our greatest response to God, and the core message of the kingdom. A loving relationship with God is foundational to every aspect of the kingdom.

It is the primary grid through which we **define:**

⚬ theology, salvation, justice,

⚬ the Great Commission, the glory of God, the supremacy of Jesus,

⚬ eternal rewards, the millennial kingdom, judgment,

⚬ the Body of Christ, worship, intercession,

⚬ holiness, humility, faith,

⚬ family life, economic prosperity, leadership.   (Mike Bickle)

1 John 3:1

*See how **great** a **love** the Father has bestowed on us,
that we would be called children of God; and such we are.*

Streaming *in* Heaven's Flow

Because of Love

Love, Intimacy and Encountering God

Jeremiah 31:3

> *The LORD appeared to him from afar, saying,*
>   *"I have loved you with an **everlasting love**;*
>   *Therefore I have drawn you with lovingkindness."*

I. It Is Because of Love

A. Love is the True Motivator

B. The call to work in prayer and intercession has to be preceded by our love for God and our love for people.

1) Streaming in Heaven's Flow, using worship, intercession and music as weapons is vitally important.

2) We should do it and enter into it because of a greater understanding for His love for us.

II. This is Our Baseline

A. We pray and do worship because of the power of knowing God intimately.

B. We were created for His pleasure.

C. Love released bears great fruit.

III. There is No Fear in the Perfect Love of God

A. Fear is an evil taskmaster. Fear produces:

1) lack of confidence

2) insecurity,

3) nightmares

4) a certain withdrawal from reality.

B. Love produces

    1) strength,

    2) hope,

    3) faith,

    4) joy,

    5) ongoing endurance.

C. Perfect love casts out, annihilates, and makes fear go away.

IV. Learning the Deeper Realm of Intimacy

A. Motivation for "Streaming in Heaven's Flow"

For a life to be given fully to worship, prayer and music, there has to be a greater understanding of intimacy with God and His desire to be with us.

V. Encounters with Jesus

A. Forgiveness

B. Healing - Restoration

C. Revelation and Light

D. The Eternal Encounter - the Cross

VI. Love: The Core Message of the Kingdom

A. Love is

    1) the greatest virtue

    2) our greatest response to God

    3) the core message of the kingdom

        Loving relationship with God is foundational to every aspect of the kingdom.

1 John 3:1

*See how **great** a **love** the Father has bestowed on us,*
*   that we would be called children of God; and such we are.*

Every Believer's Eternal Identity

*For we will function as priests in a
holy priesthood even in eternity!
When this concept of
priesthood becomes a
reinforced reality in our hearts,
we are stronger and more effective
in music, worship and intercession.*

*"You are . . . a royal priesthood
for this reason . . . to show forth
the wonderful deeds and
display the virtues and perfections of Him
Who called you out of darkness
into His marvelous light. "*

Chapter Five

Every Believer's Eternal Identity

Royal Priests unto the Lord

I Peter 2: 9

> *But you are A CHOSEN GENERATION ,*
> *A royal PRIESTHOOD,   A HOLY NATION,*
> *A (peculiar) PEOPLE FOR*
> *God's OWN POSSESSION,*
> *so that you may proclaim the excellencies*
> *(perfections) of Him*
> *who has called you out of darkness into*
> *His marvelous light;*

[The words capitalized in this scripture represent the restating of Old Testament scriptures.

> Exodus 19:6 . . . "and you shall be to Me a **kingdom** of **priests** and a 'holy nation.' These are the words that you shall speak to the sons of Israel."]

Every Believer is Part of God's Priesthood

This is a Biblical principle we should all study and we must know: Proverbs 23:7 says *"as a man thinks in his heart, so is he."*

As much as possible, we need to learn what the Bible says about us and we need to believe who the Bible says we are in Christ. The understanding of our identity as believers is super important. If we are believing things about ourselves that are contrary to the Bible, we would want to change those things, right?

73

So the Scripture records the importance of our earthly destiny but clearly states that we all have an eternal identity in Christ. We are all part of **His Royal Priesthood**.

A Kingly Priesthood

> *But you are A CHOSEN GENERATION,*
> > *A Royal [Kingly] PRIESTHOOD . . .* (IPeter 2:9)

A Kingdom of Priests

> *"You have made them to be a kingdom and priests to our God;*
> *and they will reign upon the earth."* (Revelation 5:10)

A Spiritual House of Holy Priests

> *You also, as living stones,*
> > *are being built up as a spiritual house for a*
> *holy priesthood, to offer up spiritual sacrifices acceptable to*
> *God through Jesus Christ.* (1Peter 2:5)

Our Dilemma, Our Challenge

Our dilemma is how do we get the people of Destiny Church, mostly not given to regular prayer, to start praying at higher levels? How can we help people really comprehend the importance of prayer and worship especially as God designed it? And that is we are co-laborers with Him, so as we do prayer and worship, His will is being done and His Kingdom is coming.

We must know that
priesthood is our
God-given, eternal identity in Christ.

For we will function as priests in a holy priesthood even in eternity! It is said that the simplest Christian praying makes hell take notice. When this concept of priesthood becomes a reinforced reality in our hearts, we are stronger and more effective in music, worship and intercession.

In my home church in St. Louis, (Destiny Church), we had to figure out the major teaching points that would help our church cross over into becoming a Praying Church. For the most part, we were unconvinced of the importance of prayer.

So we began combining live music with deeper worship and then adding prayer layered on top of these two. It is a match made in Heaven as we will learn later in this book.

There is a great need to help people understand that they have a higher spiritual calling. This call to prayer and worship goes far beyond mere church attendance and fulfilling a weekly obligation.

This is why we started teaching the truth about the **priestly identity** of every believer. It causes us to have greater light and revelation of who we are and why we pray and worship. It is such a large part of our walk with the Lord on the earth.

Our Identity in Christ: the Four Major Parts

In the second chapter of First Peter, verse 9, there is a plain, yet simple truth. It is easy to remember and full of revelation. We are part of a community that is very spiritual; the Body of Christ is defined in four parts.

We are a **chosen** people, selected by the Lord Himself.

We are the King's priests, part of His royal **priesthood**.

We are to live as a **holy** nation, in the world but not of it.

We are the people that belong to God. He made us His own special people. He claimed us as **His own possession**.   (ERV)

I Peter 2:9-10

> [9] *But you are A CHOSEN GENERATION (RACE) ,*
> *A royal PRIESTHOOD, A HOLY NATION,*
> *A PEOPLE FOR **God's OWN POSSESSION**,*
> *[God's] own purchased, special people,* (AMP)
>
> *so that you may proclaim the excellencies*
> *(the perfections) of Him*
>
> *that you may set forth the wonderful deeds and display the virtues and perfections of Him Who called you out of darkness into His marvelous light.* (AMP)
>
> [10] *for you once were NOT A PEOPLE, but now you are THE PEOPLE OF GOD; you had NOT RECEIVED MERCY, but now you have RECEIVED MERCY.*

75

My chosen people: a special classification of believers

> *"The beasts of the field will glorify Me, the jackals and the ostriches, because I have given waters in the wilderness and rivers in the desert, to give drink to **My chosen people**."*
> (Isaiah 43:20)

Royal Priesthood: priests of the Lord, ministers of our God

> *But you will be called the **priests** of the **LORD**;*
> *You will be spoken of as **ministers** of our **God**.*
> *You will eat the wealth of nations, and in their riches you will boast.* (Isaiah 61:6)

Holy Nation: living and walking as a kingdom of priests

> 5 *Now then, if you will indeed obey My voice and keep My covenant, then you shall be **My own possession** among all the peoples, for all the earth is Mine;*
>
> 6 *and you shall be to Me a **kingdom of priests** and a **holy nation**. These are the words that you shall speak to the sons of Israel.* (Exodus 19:5-6)

You're God's: we are His own purchased, special people:

> *Who gave Himself for us to redeem us from every lawless deed, and to purify for Himself a people for **His** own **possession**, zealous for good deeds.* (Titus 2:14)

CHOSEN GENERATION

First, we are a **CHOSEN GENERATION.** The dictionary definition of generation is:

a *RACE - (or tribe)* of people **united by blood** or custom; a select, ["elected by God" people] operating for a limited time in human history.

The word chosen - eklektos - (ek-lek-to's) means to be picked out, chosen by God, selected, (i.e. the best of its kind or class).

Generation - genos - (ge'-nos) is defined as the aggregate of many individuals of the same nature, kind, or sort, offspring, family, tribe or nation.

So we can say that a praying church is many people, united by the Blood of Jesus, who gather together with a common goal. It is to do the priestly ministry of prayer and worship, to pray, "Your Kingdom come, Your will be done" and to bind and overcome the kingdom of darkness.

Royal Priesthood and Kingly Ministers

Second, the scripture calls you a **Royal Priesthood**. You were made to serve in the inner courts of your King. You are in a **special group** of priests set apart to **minister first** to God as Lord and King. If you believe in the Lord Jesus Christ, this is your eternal job description.

You will be ministering to the Lord forever. This life is but a vapor and yet all prayer and worship rises as incense and makes a difference in the spirit realm.

Your spiritual service of worship according to Romans 12 verses 1 and 2 is**:**

> *Therefore, I urge you, brethren, by the mercies of God,*
> *to present your bodies a living and holy sacrifice,*
> *acceptable (well-pleasing) to God,*
> *which is **your spiritual service of worship**.*

In the Message translation, Romans 12:1-2 says this:

> *So here's what I want you to do, God helping you:*

❖ Your Life, a Special Offering

> *Take your everyday, ordinary life - your sleeping,*
> *eating, going-to-work, and walking-around life -*
> *and **place it** before God **as an offering**.*

❖ Fix Your Attention on God

> *Don't become so well-adjusted to your culture that you fit into*
> *it without even thinking.*
> *Instead, fix your attention on God.*
> *You'll be changed from the inside out.*
>
> *Readily recognize what He wants from you,*
> *and quickly respond to it.*

❖ Developing Well-formed Maturity

> *Unlike the culture around you, always dragging you down*

to its level of immaturity (carnal things, fleshly pursuits),

God brings the best out of you, develops well-formed maturity in you. Do not be conformed to this world (age),
but be transformed by the renewing of your mind.

❖ Transformed by God into a New Person

Don't copy the behavior and customs of this world, but let God transform you into a new person by changing the way you think. Then you will know what God wants you to do and you will know how good and pleasing and perfect His will really is.

(NLT)

A Holy Nation Who Reveres the Lord

The third point in First Peter 2:9 is that
we are a ***Holy Nation***.

The designation of **"holy"** allows us to do a special work. Again, every Christ-believer is called to walk in holiness. No one gets an exemption and everyone is accountable. We are all "living epistles read of all men."

2Corinthians 3:2 *You are our letter, written in our hearts, known and read by all men;*

One of the very first preachers we ever had at my first church, was very comical and yet very profound. He made this statement back in 1975 but I have never forgotten it:

"The world is not reading their Bibles,
they are reading their Christians."

Holy is a misunderstood word. Holy is an attitude of heart. It's the pursuit of the higher things of God concerning purity and the state of right living. As you develop this attitude of heart, your worldly desires for sin fade away and you long for the things that God longs for in His heart.

Holy - hagios - (hä'-gē-os) is defined "on account of His incomparable majesty"; [Exodus 15:11 - majestic in His own holiness], one who is perfect in goodness and righteousness; which makes us full of reverence, full of awe.

Nation - ethnos - (e'-thnos) is a multitude of people associated or living together; a company, troop, or a tribe with a territory, economic life, distinctive culture, and **language** in common.

Let us walk with godly virtues as a HOLY NATION of people full of the reverence for who God is; adoring the Person of the Lord Jesus, worshipping His majesty and living in awe of Him. By doing this we will live better because of holiness and be a church that hears the heartbeat of God. Then prayer becomes a daily natural outflow of our hearts.

A Special People for God's Own Possession

Fourth, the scripture calls us, His Church, **a special people** *for His own possession,* purchased for God by His Son.

We are a **people** – laos – (lä-o's) a group, tribe, nation, those who are of the same stock and language gathered together.

We are His **possession -** peripoiēsis –(pe-rē-poi'-ā-sēs) - a preserving, a preservation of His property. The preserving of a soul that is the saving of a soul that it may be made a partaker of eternal salvation; a possession, one's own property.

(Thayer's Lexicon)

We are the Lord's property that truly makes us a set-apart, special people. The scripture I Peter 2:9 gives us the reason for this position.

"You are . . . a royal priesthood . . .
for this reason, . . .
to show forth the wonderful deeds and
display the virtues and perfections of Him
Who called you out of darkness
into His marvelous light." (AMP)

We were purchased by the Blood to show forth His perfections, to display His virtues. We are living testimonies of the goodness of God. As I stated earlier, we have to change our mindset and believe that we can and do make a difference in people's lives by prayer and being an example.

The Forever Priesthood

Hebrews 7:1-3   The extraordinary facts
                         recorded about King Melchizedek

> ¹ *For this Melchizedek, king of Salem,* **priest** *of the Most High God, who met Abraham as he was returning from the slaughter of the kings and blessed him,*
>
> ² *to whom also Abraham apportioned a tenth part (tithe) of all the spoils, was first of all, by the translation of his name,* **king** *of* **righteousness***, and then also* **king** *of* **Salem***, which is* **king** *of* **peace***.*
>
> ³ *Without father, without mother, without genealogy, having neither beginning of days nor end of life,*
>   *but made like the Son of God,*
>   *he remains* **a priest perpetually***.*

Back in Genesis chapter 14, Melchizedek came to meet Abram (later called, Abraham) after his victory over the five kings. The reason that Abram actually went up to war was that his nephew, Lot, was kidnapped from Sodom and Gomorrah by the five kings.

Abram was a tremendous man of war. He had trained 318 of his servants as his personal army. They were special operations, delta force and navy seals before any one knew what that was. They could wield the sword, shoot their bows and use their shields. They were super stealthy. Here's the point, if you are going to steal someone's nephew, you would want to avoid taking Abram's.

So as Abram came back from his great victory, the king, Melchizedek came to Abram and gave him bread and wine and blessed him. Abram paid Melchizedek a tenth of all of his spoils of war which we understand today is the tithe or the tenth.

Genesis 14:18-20

> ¹⁸ *And* **Melchizedek,** *king of* **Salem** *brought out bread and wine; now he was a* **priest** *of God Most High.*
> ¹⁹ *He blessed Abram and said, "Blessed be Abram of God Most High, Possessor of heaven and earth;*
> ²⁰ *And blessed be God Most High, Who has delivered your enemies into your hand." He gave him a tenth of all.*

As the identity of Melchizedek unfolds in Genesis 14, it is then restated in Hebrews 7. We perceive from these scriptures that Melchizedek could have been Jesus Himself appearing in time. The reason for Jesus' appearing was to establishing our ongoing human need of priesthood. Jesus is being the mediator between God Himself and man.

Also, Jesus did establish the forever priesthood at His rising from the dead, ascending into Heaven and sprinkling His Blood on the heavenly ornaments. He provided a new and living way into the presence of Almighty God.

He understood that New Testament believers would need a forerunner who was a priest as an example. This provided the means for New Testament believers to follow His lead as the Eternal Priest. We would then be able to flow in the priestly ministry of praise and worship because of Him.

The Meaning of the Name of Melchizedek

Look at the attributes and meaning of Melchizedek, the king of Salem, from his person and his name:

* His name translated means the "king of righteousness."

* Further, he was referred to as the king of Salem, which literally means the "king of peace."

  [Only Jesus is referred to by these names in both Testaments. There is no other king that has ever been known by these names individually or the combination of the two.]

* This king was without father and without mother and even without genealogy. The question is, "how is this even possible?"

  Has there ever been a king on the earth, without father or mother? No, there has never been one. So Melchizedek's appearing in Genesis 14 is important for this main reason.

It began the ministry of the priest and the priesthood unto the Most High God. The Priesthood of every believer has always been God's idea and intention, since He was seeking a people that He could dwell with and live in as His vessels.

Hebrews 7:15-17, 23-25

A Priest FOREVER, He holds His priesthood permanently.

¹⁵ *And this is clearer still, if another priest arises according to the likeness of Melchizedek,*

¹⁶ *who has become not (a priest) on the basis of a law of physical requirement, [fleshly commandment; i.e. to be a descendant of Levi] but according to the power of an **indestructible life**.*

¹⁷ *For it is attested of Him,*
*"YOU ARE A **PRIEST FOREVER** ACCORDING TO THE ORDER OF MELCHIZEDEK."*

²³ *The former priests, on the one hand, existed in greater numbers because they **were prevented by death** from continuing,*

²⁴ *but Jesus, on the other hand, because He continues forever, holds His priesthood permanently.*

²⁵ *Therefore He is able also to save forever those who draw near to God through Him, since **He always lives** to **make intercession** for them.*

Our Example: Jesus as the Merciful and Faithful High Priest, He is the Mighty Intercessor.

Think about this!
Priesthood and priestly ministry do not go away in eternity.

It is the ministry we **continue to do** in Heaven and it is forever. This Priesthood is established by Jesus Himself, through His sacrifice and resurrection.

Our Lord's Priesthood is fixed because of

*. . . the power of an indestructible life. For it is attested of Him, " YOU ARE A **PRIEST FOREVER** according TO THE ORDER OF MELCHIZEDEK."* Hebrews 7:17

The problem with the priesthood in the Old Testament was the priests kept dying. Jesus changed this fact through His death and resurrection. Now He lives forever. Death is no longer an issue. We, as His priests step from this life on earth into our eternal life.

We are His people that function as a "kingdom of priests." We have a special place, position and function.

Jesus **saved** us ... to live as a people redeemed from our sins, walking in new life.

Jesus **made** us ... to be His people that **function** as His "kingdom of priests."

It is a position of power to intervene in real time, through prayer, worship, music and intercession. We are using the dynamic of priestly ministry before Him to honor Him through worship with intercession.

The Sacred "Doings" of the Priest: "Sacerdotal" Duties

Jesus made us a "kingdom of priests," **to minister**. First, to minister to God, to know His heart, His will and His purposes. Second to **do the ministry** He does, He ever lives to make intercession.

> **Sacerdotal : The sacred duties ...** pertaining to the priesthood.

Minister means to serve, to wait on or to attend to. It is one who serves at the altar or one who performs **sacerdotal** duties.

Sacerdotal: pertaining to priests or priesthood, the **sacred** duties ... the function of a priest, having sacerdotal (priestly) character.

Noah Webster defines minister as "one to whom the king entrusts the direction of His affairs of state, a chief servant, an agent appointed to transact business under the authority of another." [Noah Webster 1828 - Am. Dict. of the English Lang.]

That says it all. As Priests, we have the Name of Jesus. Jesus trusts us with His affairs. We are His agents, appointed to go about His business on the earth just as He was here doing His Father's business. So what is a believer's true identity? It is not your earthly identity. **Every** believer's "Eternal" Identity is a priest, and we are part of a kingly priesthood.

We have a high calling of priestly work. We should be Priests that carry His heart and know how to worship and intercede. We have the ability to pray change into our world. Do you think Jesus prays prayers that won't be answered? We know that they will be answered.

He prayed in John 17:11
(which NAS calls the High Priestly Prayer),

". . . that they (His disciples) may be one even as We (the Father, Jesus and the Holy Spirit) are one." If that happens and it will, since Jesus is the High Priest, we will all be priests.

The Body of Christ also has a **priestly ministry.** It is to be God's people "engaged" in deeper worship and while doing effective, enjoyable prayer, living lifestyles pleasing to the Lord. How long will this calling last? It is the Forever Priesthood established by Jesus Himself.

The Priestly Ministry of Prayer and Worship

Priests in the Old Testament tended to the King, tended to the fire and the altar it dwelt on, and tended to their own relationship with God.

They were chosen by God for the high calling of priestly work. They were chosen to be a holy people and God's instruments to do His work and speak out for Him. They had to live a consecrated life before the Lord while sustaining the ability to bless and pray for people.

A consecrated life is described in IPeter 2:1 -3

"Therefore, rid yourselves of all malice, of all deceit, hypocrisy and envy, and of all the ways there are of speaking against people; and be like newborn babies, thirsty for the pure milk of the Word; so that by it, you may grow up into deliverance. For you have tasted that ADONAI is good."

Malice - active ill-will; desire to harm another; spite; animosity; hate; ill-feeling; hostility; grudge

Deceit - act of representing as true what is known to be false; a deceiving or lying; DISHONESTY

Hypocrisy - pretended sanctity; acting a part; false guise; hollowness

Envy - having hatred or ill-will; jealousy; resentment; covetousness

We need to rid our lives of these four things even if our goal is only to have a better life. So why not do it for an eternal purpose? Every believer is called to a priestly lifestyle. I Peter 2:5 says, we are living stones, being built up as a **spiritual** house for a holy **priesthood**, to offer up **spiritual** sacrifices acceptable to God through Jesus Christ.

This scripture defines the priestly ministry of the Body of Christ. We are a Priesthood that ministers **to** the King, **before** the King and **alongside** the King (Jesus).

As a Kingdom of priests, we function as His people.

Revelation 5:10 says,

"Jesus made us a 'kingdom of priests' to our God and we will reign upon the earth."

We can intervene **with Him** in the affairs of God and man, with hearts on fire, through our prayers, worship, music and intercessions!!

A Spiritual House for a Holy Priesthood

First Peter, chapter two becomes your starting point. You are called to be a **spiritual house** for a **holy priesthood.** To become a spiritual house, you need to spend time in His presence. The amount of time you spend in His presence directly correlates to the strength of your house.

For example, the more time you invest wisely in personal relationships, truly the richer you become in friendship and love. The same principle applies here. The more time you spend with Him, the more of Him, His wisdom and character you receive. The amount of time you are willing to invest is up to you.

IPeter 2:4-8

[4] *And coming to Him as to a living stone, which has been rejected by men, but is choice [elect, chosen] and precious in the sight of God,*

85

⁵ *y-o-u a-l-s-o, as **living stones**, are being built up as a spiritual **house** for a holy **priesthood**,*
   *to offer up **spiritual** sacrifices acceptable to God through Jesus Christ.*

⁶ *For this is contained in Scripture, "Behold! I lay in Zion a choice stone, a precious cornerstone;*
   and he who believes in Him shall not be disappointed."

⁷ *This precious value, then, is for you who believe, but for those who disbelieve, The Stone (Jesus) which the builders rejected, This became the very Cornerstone;"* (NAS)

⁸ *also He is a stone that will make people stumble, a rock over which they will trip. They are stumbling at the Word, disobeying it - as had been planned.* (CJB)

The priestly ministry of everyday believers is to be living stones and care for each other and the lost in this dying world. We should be building each other up, encouraging one another. This is why a developed prayer and worship life is so necessary to bless and minister to others.

⁴ *You are coming to Christ, who is the living Cornerstone of God's temple. He was rejected by people, but He was chosen by God for great honor.*

⁵ *And you are living stones that God is building into His spiritual temple. What's more, you are **His holy priests** through the mediation of Jesus Christ, you offer spiritual sacrifices that please God.* (NLT)

Offerings in the Holy Spirit

This is what He said we would do . . . making offerings in the Holy Spirit. He would have us as His . . . friends, bride and army!! We are to serve as priests unto the Lord, acting as God's care-givers (helpers) to all people.

IPeter 2:4

*You, as living stones, are being made into a house of the Spirit, a holy order of priests, making those **offerings of the spirit** which are pleasing to God through Jesus Christ.* (BBE)

Spiritual offerings are simply our music, our worship, and our prayers. These all become a type of spiritual warfare. When we use our voice, when we use our mind and when we engage our spirit, the Lord is glorified and change comes in the earth.

We have been given the most valuable and powerful tool. The Living Word, set to music, sung from hearts on fire, is a pure, righteous, spiritual force!!

Isaiah 55:10-11

[10] *For as the rain and the snow come down from heaven,*
       and do not return there without
    watering *the earth and **making** it bear and sprout, and*
    furnishing *seed to the sower and bread to the eater;*

[11] *So will My word be which goes forth from My mouth;*
       *It will not return to Me **empty**,*
    *Without **accomplishing** what I desire,*
       and without succeeding in the matter for which I sent it.

[11] *The same thing is true of the words I speak. They will not return to Me empty. In the same way, My words leave My mouth, and they don't come back until they make things happen.*
My words make the things happen that I want to happen.
My words succeed in doing the things I send them to do.
                                                (NCV, ERV)

The Lord set this in His creation as an irrefutable point! We have **stored-up, transforming power** of the Word of God available to us. When the people of God begin to sing and pray the Scriptures, it releases the stored-up power that is in the Word of God.

As the power in the Word of God comes forth [by singing it and praying it] it becomes transforming **power** that changes the spiritual atmosphere and the condition of our hearts.

Again, if Jesus said it, it will come to pass! His words are powerful. He created all things by speaking them into existence. He is the same yesterday, TODAY, and forever. He still creates with His words and so do we. So it is our place and call as priests to minister to those the Lord has placed in our lives.

Every believer's true identity is to function as a priest unto the Lord. We are kingly priests before the Lord. Our eternal identity is not bank teller, medical sales rep, or Wal-Mart Sales associate. We, the people of God, are called to do the priestly ministry of prayer and worship. We are God's instruments to do His work and speak out for Him. He has chosen to work with us as His partners.

The Promise of a House of Prayer for All Peoples

Isaiah 56:6-7

[6] *Also the foreigners who (a) **join themselves** to the LORD,
(b) **to minister** to Him, and (c) **to love the name** of the LORD,
(d) and to **be** His **servants**,
every one who keeps from profaning the Sabbath and holds
fast My covenant; (things that release His power & holiness);*

[7] *Even those I will bring to My holy mountain
and make them **joyful in My house of prayer**.*

*Their burnt offerings and their sacrifices will be **acceptable**
on My altar; For My house will be called
a house of prayer for all the peoples.*

These scriptures reveal that even the Gentiles, the foreigners will be welcome to worship the same as the "insiders," (the Hebrew believers) on God's holy mountain. The mission and purpose of the House of Prayer is building joyful worship and prayer everywhere; Oh yes, My house of worship will be known as a house of prayer for **all** people. "I will make My people joyful in My House of Prayer," declares the Lord

In our cities and nations we are a part of a global prayer movement that will cover the earth. Is there not a cause? Our cause is The House of Prayer where worshipping intercessors are operating before the Lord. The prayer room culture, vision and values is where the Kingly Priesthood is operating.

Streaming in Heaven's Flow

Every Believer's Eternal Identity

Royal Priests unto the Lord

I. **Every Believer is Part of God's Priesthood** - I Peter 2: 9

We must know that priesthood is our God-given, eternal identity in Christ.

A. A Kingly Priesthood . . . a kingdom of priests,
. . . a spiritual house of Holy Priests (I Peter 2:5-9)

B. For we will function as priests in a holy priesthood even in eternity. Our priestly identity causes us to have greater light and revelation of who we are and why we pray and worship.

II. **Our Identity in Christ: the Four Major Parts**

We are a **chosen** people, selected by the Lord Himself.

We are the King's priests, part of His royal **priesthood**.

We are to live as a **holy** nation, in the world but not of it.

We are the people that belong to God. He made us His own special people. He claimed us as **His own possession**. (ERV)

A. Chosen

We can say that a praying church is many people, united by the Blood of Jesus, who gather together with a common goal.

B. Royal Priesthood

1) You were made to serve in the inner courts of our King.
2) Worship and prayer is your spiritual service of worship.

C. Holy Nation

You develop a greater understanding of what holiness is. Your worldly desires for sin fade away and you long for the things that God longs for in His heart.

D. His Own Possession

We were purchased by the Blood to show forth His perfections, to display His virtues. We are living testimonies of the goodness of God.

III. The Forever Priesthood

Hebrews 7 : 2-3

[2] *... (Melchizedek) king of **righteousness**, and then also king of **Salem**, which is king of **peace**.*

[3] *Without father, without mother, without genealogy, having neither beginning of days nor end of life, but made like the Son of God, he remains a **priest perpetually**.*

A. The Attributes and Meaning of Melchizedek

1) His name translated means the "king of righteousness."

2) Further, he was referred to as the king of Salem, which literally means the "king of peace."

Only Jesus is referred to by these names in both Testaments.

3) This king was without father and without mother and even without genealogy. (For a normal king, this is not humanly possible.)

IV. The Priestly Ministry of Prayer and Worship

A. Every believer is called to a priestly lifestyle. I Peter 2:5 says, we are living stones, being built up as a **spiritual** house for a holy **prlesthood**, to offer up **spiritual** sacrifices acceptable to God through Jesus Christ.

B. Offerings in the Holy Spirit

Spiritual offerings are simply our music, our worship, and our prayers. These all become a type of spiritual warfare.
We have been given the most valuable and powerful tool. The Living Word, set to music, sung from hearts on fire, is a pure, righteous, spiritual force!!

V. The Promise of a House of Prayer for All Peoples

Isaiah 56:7 Joyful in My House of Prayer

In our cities, nations we are a part of a global prayer movement that will cover the earth. The House of Prayer is where worshipping intercessors are ministering before the Lord. The prayer room culture, vision and values is where the Kingly Priesthood is operating

"Intercession, the Power to Intervene"

"Those who partner with God,
to bring about His will
and Kingdom on the earth,
are shaping the future
through prayer and intercession."

Everyone is called to pray
and intercede as Jesus does
with "fiery prayer and effectual power."
He is saying,
"Come and join Me as co-laborers
in prayer and intercession."

Chapter Six

"Intercession,
The Power to Intervene"

Living as His People of Prayer and Worship

Ezekiel 22:29-31

> God is looking for someone to stand up for what's right.

29 *"The people of the land have: practiced oppression and committed robbery, and they have wronged the poor and needy and have oppressed the sojourner without justice."*

30 *"**I searched** for **a man** among them who would **make up the hedge** (KJV) and **stand in the gap before Me** for the land, so that I would not destroy it; but I found no one (not one)."*

30 *"I looked for someone to stand up for Me against all this (injustice) to repair the defenses of the city, to take a stand for Me*

   . . . and stand in the gap to protect this land so I wouldn't have to destroy it.
      I couldn't find anyone. Not one." (MSG)

31 *"Thus I have poured out My indignation on them; I have consumed them with the fire of My wrath; their way I have brought upon their heads," declares the Lord GOD.*

History Belongs to the Intercessor

I visited a church in Littleton, Colorado to lead a Night of Worship. Upon arriving early in the afternoon, the doors were locked. I looked in the front window. On the archway going into the sanctuary, in bold block letters, it said,

I was astonished and stood amazed at this statement. It changed my life forever, for it summed up what I had come to believe was the Lord's heart for every believer. Everyone is called to **"pray more"** and worship more. We will pray consistently until we see a greater release of the Lord's anointing which brings His help and His justice on the earth.

What is Intercession?

The answer is simple. It is prayer from your heart. You stand in the gap for friends, family and people who have a need. You run interference for them spiritually. Intercession is the ability to intervene into someone's situation with the power of God to bring change. God is looking for partners.

> "Those who partner with God,
> to bring about His will and Kingdom
> on the earth,
> are **shaping** the **future**
> through prayer and intercession."
>
> (Carla Henry, my wife)

The real understanding of intercession is found in the Hebrew language and it is as clear as a bell: to **intercede** - to intervene; to pray; mediate (act as a go-between).

Intervene and Step In

Intercession and prayer take guts, courage, time and a certain selflessness. Here we are, in the Lord, able to intercede and intervene while covered with His awesome protection:

His Name,   His Blood . . .
    the power of His life as the crucified Lamb of God.

So, we can step in; make a willful decision to insert ourselves. The word intercession in the Hebrew Language is *palal, (*pä·lal') which means to interpose as mediator. More easily understood, a person who engages in prayer. They do so by placing themselves in an intervening position as a liaison, troubleshooter or bargainer.

Further, intercession means to "get involved, interject, (squeeze in, get between)." Aren't these phrases amazing? This truly defines the heart of those who carry out the priestly ministry of prayer and worship.

Israel Pleads for an Intercessor

Because of intercession, disaster can be averted. By someone engaged in prayer, tragedy can be turned away. The result of intercession should give us a clue to the importance of the life surrendered to God, living near to His heart. When we choose to pray and worship, we are living in a place where we can be a mouthpiece of the Lord, praying here on the earth.

The Lord introduced the element of intercession early in the Bible. It must be of great value since He brought it forth in the Old Testament. It is in the Pentateuch which are the first five books of the Bible written by Moses, (the same as the Jewish Torah).

Numbers 21:4-7

The people of God are impatient in their journey through the desert, and of course they start complaining big-time. The Lord sent serpents in their midst for the sin of disrespect. Realizing their sin, they said to Moses . . .

*"We have sinned, because we have spoken against the LORD and you; **intercede with the LORD**, that He may remove the serpents from us,"*
*and **Moses interceded** for the people.*

The **Situation:** (verse 4) - *"Then the Israelites set out from Mount Hor by the way of the Red Sea, to go around the land of Edom; and the people became **impatien**t because of the journey."*

Other translations say, *"The soul of the people was short, people complaining again."*

The **Attitude:** (verse 5) - *The people spoke against God and Moses, "Why have you brought us up out of Egypt to die in the wilderness? For there is no food and no water, and we loathe this miserable food."*

They were accusatory in nature and disrespectful of authority.

> Loathe: to dislike greatly and often with disgust or intolerance, to detest

[The word loathe by its very nature reveals the attitude of their heart in that moment.]

The **Judgment:** (verse 6) - *The LORD sent fiery serpents among the people and they bit the people, so that many people of Israel died.*

Old Testament judgment was seemingly very severe, but the Lord knew the importance of obedience and the right heart attitude. These two things define the degree of the people's blessing.

The **Remedy:** (verse 7) - *So the people came to Moses and said, "We have sinned, because we have spoken against the LORD and you, **intercede** * **with the Lord**, that He may remove the serpents from us," and **Moses interceded** for the people.*

(*intercede: this is the first time this word appears in the Bible and it happens twice in the same verse.)

I Samuel 2:25

*If one man sins against another, God will mediate for him; but if a man sins against the LORD, who can **intercede** for him? "But they would not listen to the voice of their father . . . "*

Intercession is the Power to Intervene

God is looking for someone to stand up for what is right and realize that intercession is the power to intervene. As intercessors, we can pray and disaster is averted. We need do what Jesus is doing in Heaven and enter into the ministry of intercession (Hebrews 7:25). We will discuss this later in this chapter.

I have two friends who live in St. Louis that met every Friday to pray for St. Louis. One afternoon they were praying about the violence in the streets of our city to cease. Their prayer was, "No death, No death, No death." They were following the leading of the Holy Spirit to pray this prayer over downtown St. Louis.

As they drove around the city proclaiming "No death," they were unaware of an approaching storm that produced a tornado in another part of the city. Miles of the city suburbs were destroyed but the National News Headlines the next day were: Miracle in St. Louis, NO DEATH!

Not one person died. Disaster was averted. The Lord used these two ladies as a mouthpiece in that moment to declare the Word of God which made a difference in real time.

Always remember there is no such thing as unanswered prayer. The answer or result may be delayed or hindered but God hears the cry of the righteous. The answer you receive may not be the one you are expecting but God has still answered.

Numbers 21 gives us a crucial, giant revelation: the working knowledge that intercession is always an available option that should be pursued. It is a powerful precedent (example) that this man, Moses, could do intercession with a Holy God, who is both judge and jury.

It is possible to . . . intercede with the Lord, to intervene in the affairs of God and man. It is possible to . . . step in between, mediate, and change the outcome by righteous intercession.

We can not just stand by and do nothing. We must act in the power of the Holy Spirit's leadership. We have been given life's breath to activate and release God's help through His saving power. It is a privilege and now it is **a right** and **responsibility** (working through prayer), praying prayers of justice, releasing the Word of God and the judgments written within.

God is Looking for Someone to Stand Up for
What is Right

Ezekiel 22:29-31

[29] *The people of the land have:*
practiced oppression and committed robbery, and they have

wronged the poor and needy and have oppressed the sojourner without justice.

[30] *"**I searched** for **a man** among them who would*
make up the hedge   (KJV)
*and **stand in the gap before Me** for the land, so that I would not destroy it; but I found no one (not one)."*

[30] *"I looked for someone to stand up for Me against all this (injustice) to repair the defenses of the city, to take a stand for Me*
. . . and stand in the gap to protect this land so I wouldn't have to destroy it."

I couldn't find anyone. Not one. (MSG)

[31] *"Thus I have poured out My indignation on them; I have consumed them with the fire of My wrath; their way I have brought upon their heads," declares the Lord GOD.*

Four Major Points

God First Searched for a Man   "I searched."

The Lord is **still** looking for men, women, teenagers, and "*tweeners*" who will pray. The Lord longs for a people who He can draw to Himself and work through.

"Who?"   People who are wiling to "go to work."

We can go to work in prayer, worship, and intercession for the good of others. So it is time that the Body of Christ takes their place with the Head of the Church, Jesus, and joins Him in intercession.

The Power to Bless

We have the ability to **bless with our tongue.** There is much power in a consecrated tongue. This is what we use as we do spiritual warfare. That's what "making a hedge is." You surround people with prayer.

Proverbs 18:20-21 says,

With the fruit [speech] of a man's mouth, his stomach will be satisfied; He will be satisfied with the product of his lips.

Death and life are in the power of the tongue, and those who love it (indulge it) will eat its fruit.

Words kill, words give life.
   They're either poison or fruit - - you choose. (MSG)

Those who love to talk will experience the consequences, for the tongue can kill or nourish life. (NLT)

Standing in the Gap

Every believer should be "making up the hedge while **standing in the gap**," praying and singing the Word of God for the help of others. We have the honor of living a prayer-filled, lifestyle full of worship. So, God is still searching for someone. Who is He looking for? It is **You.**

Bless people with your tongue, pray a hedge around them and stand in the gap. This is intercession.

The New Testament Fulfillment of Ezekiel 22:30

Ephesians 6:18

With all prayer and petition, pray at all times in the Spirit, and with this in view, be on the alert with all perseverance (unwearied persistence) and petition for all the saints.

One: Pray at all times;
   becomes a lifestyle through out the day . . .

Pray at all times (on every occasion, in every season) in the Spirit, with all [manner of] prayer and entreaty. To that end, keep alert and watch with strong purpose and perseverance, interceding on behalf of all the saints (God's consecrated people).
(AMP)

This is doable for people in any walk of life. It is like having a CB radio on. There is an open channel in your spirit that you can sense the leading of the Holy Spirit and pray out of that.

Two: Be on the alert to pray,
   "to seize opportunities for doing so,"

In the same way, prayer is essential in this ongoing warfare. (MSG)

Pray with unceasing prayer and entreaty . . . and be always on the alert to seize opportunities for doing so, with unwearied persistence and entreaty on behalf of all God's people. (WNT)

I find that people have very little focus on the Lord as they go about their daily life. Be on the alert means having your spiritual radar on whether at work, play or in prayer. So we should be tuned into the Lord almost in a military way where we can not be caught off guard by the schemes of the enemy.

Three: Always be ready. Never give up.
Intercede on behalf of your brothers and sisters.

Pray hard and long.
Pray for your brothers and sisters. Keep your eyes open. (MSG)

To do this you must always be ready. Never give up. (ERV)

We are relearning the effectiveness of perseverance. Sometimes life is easy and perseverance is a distant friend. Then life gets harder and the need for perseverance resurfaces. Most great people in human history and in the Bible learned the high lesson of perseverance and the full meaning of not giving up and not giving in.

God's Desire is to Have Many Intercessors

There is a direct connection between us praying in the will of God and the release of His justice on the earth. Prayer and intercession take deeper root in our hearts when the understanding that God makes wrong things right hits home.

It's fairly apparent to me now that more people would run to the place of prayer and intercession if they knew the significant results. Every breath we take and every word we speak in intercession is causing justice and righteousness to be established.

Isaiah 59:14-17

[14] ***Justice*** *is turned back, and* ***righteousness*** *stands far away;*
For ***truth*** *has stumbled in the street, and*
uprightness *cannot enter.*

[15] *Yes, truth is lacking; and he who turns aside from evil makes*
himself a prey.

Now the LORD saw, and it was displeasing in His sight that **there was no justice.**
[16] *And He saw that there was* **no man**, *and was astonished that there was* **no one to intercede;***
Then His own arm brought salvation to Him, and His righteousness upheld Him.
[17] *He put on righteousness like a breastplate, and a helmet of salvation on His head;*
and He put on garments of vengeance for clothing and wrapped Himself with **zeal as a mantle**.

This is truly a sad story unfolding in chapter 59 of Isaiah. The scripture records that God has written the Law on every mans heart. Everyone has a conscience and a sense of right and wrong. Justice was turned back and righteousness stood far away because enough people denied what they knew to be the truth concerning right and wrong.

The quote goes like this,

"All that is necessary for the triumph of evil is that good men and women do nothing."

[Edmund Burke (January 12, 1729 – July 9, 1797) was an Irish political philosopher, Whig politician and statesman who is often regarded as the father of modern conservatism.]

Concerning prayer, this is also the truth. All it takes for evil to conquer a nation is that the Christians never pray and live a life of ease and comfort.

God is Displeased that There is No Justice

In Isaiah 59, the Lord saw that truth was lacking and that there was no justice. It greatly displeased Him. In my life and heart, there is a strong sense of justice to the place that I have hated prejudice all my life. It takes so many different forms: educational prejudice, financial prejudice, skin color prejudice, wrong side of town prejudice.

So what am I to do about this? I've learned to attack it with the spirit of prayer and intercession. I know as I pray that God will change hearts and turn circumstances because He hears the cry of the righteous.

One of the great points of Isaiah 59 is verse 16. "The Lord saw that there was no man" that would be bad enough but even worse than that, God Himself was astonished that there was no one to intercede. Even in these New Testament times I want to be one of the those that removes the astonishment from the heart of the Lord.

I have signed up to be one of those who is willing to be found "Streaming in Heaven's Flow."

Sometimes our prayer and worship activities seem so weak and so futile. Not all of our Prayer Room sets turn out at level 10. Sometimes the band misses cues, singers are discombobulated and prayer leaders miss their marks.

But He records in Corinthians that His strength is made strong in our weakness. It's not our great singing. It's not our great preaching. It's not our great Hollywood type meetings. It is found with our hearts bowed down low in adoration of Him while singing and praying the Word of God, releasing this power on the earth and in the second Heavens.

2Corinthians 12:9

> And He has said to me, "My grace is sufficient for you, for power is perfected in **weakness**." (NAS)

> But He said to me, My grace (My favor and loving-kindness and mercy) is enough for you [enables you to bear the trouble manfully];
> for My strength and power are made **perfect** (fulfilled and completed) and show themselves most effective in [your] weakness.

> Therefore, I will all the more gladly glory in my weaknesses and infirmities, that the strength and power of Christ (the Messiah) may rest (yes, may pitch a tent over and dwell) upon me! (AMP)

Prayer and intercession can bring about atmospheric changes in the Spirit realm where good is overcoming evil; a city rejoices because of righteous men and women and God's justice is known by many.

Concerning Isaiah 59, since the Lord found no one to intercede, He did it Himself. This is a precedent setting scripture.

"The Lord brought salvation by His own arm.
He put on righteousness like a breastplate and the helmet of
salvation on His own head.
He put on garments of vengeance for clothing and wrapped
Himself with zeal as a mantle."

Co-Laborers with Christ in Intercession

I believe the Lord did this so that New Testament believers could enter in to the ministry that He is doing right now. He is the Chief Intercessor.

As an example, in Isaiah 59, He was a forerunner. In His earthly ministry, He was a forerunner. And now, He ever lives to make intercession for you and me. (Hebrews 7:25)

The mind-blowing fact is that He asks us to come join Him as co-laborers working with Him. It's self evident in I Corinthians 3:9. We are God's co-workers.

We are laborers together with God in major areas: the great commission, healing the sick and mending the broken, walking in the fruit and gifts of the Holy Spirit. But especially concerning intercession. He is saying "Come and join Me as co-laborers."

ICorinthians 3:9 (Paul, the Apostle, writing to the Corinthians)

*For we are fellow workmen (**laborers together**) **with** and for*
God;

you are God's garden and vineyard and field under cultivation,
[you are] God's building. (AMP)

For we are God's co-workers. You are God's field, God's building. (CSB)

For we (have) been the helpers of God; ye be the earth tilling of God, ye be the building of God. (WYC)

The invitation has been sent to every believer from the Lord to join Him in prayer until the fullness of His glory is made manifest in the whole earth. The knowledge of His glory will be seen in the whole earth. Maybe not right now. Maybe not even in our lifetime. But the scripture will come to pass.

Habakkuk 2:14

> *"For the earth will be filled with the knowledge of the glory of the LORD, as the waters cover the sea."*

2 Corinthians 4:6-7

> [6] *For God, who said, "Light shall shine out of darkness," is the One who has shone in our hearts to give the Light of the knowledge of the glory of God in the face of Christ.*

> [7] *But we have this treasure in earthen vessels, so that the surpassing greatness of the power will be of God and not from ourselves.*

Doing the Ministry that Jesus Does

We are beginning to learn more about the ministry of interceding, the power of intercession. Simply understood, an intercessor is someone who chooses to intervene, someone who steps prayerfully into the affairs of both God and man.

Hebrews 7:25

> *Therefore, He (Jesus) is able also to save forever those who draw near to God through Him, since He always lives to* **make intercession** *for them.*

> *Since He is alive forever, thus forever able to intercede, to* **intervene** *on their behalf* (AMP, CJB)

Everyone is called to pray and intercede
as Jesus does with "fiery prayer
and effectual power." He is saying,
"Come and join Me as co-laborers
in prayer and intercession."

The true fulfillment of priestly ministry is strongly tied to prayer and intercession. Doing the spiritual work of worship, singing and praying the Word of God and interceding is really the essence of the heart of a Kingdom based believer.

We are entering into the very ministry that Jesus ever lives to do now. As we learn to sing and pray the Word of God and intermingle worship with intercession, it becomes an awesome experience. We will marvel at how the presence of the Lord supports us and the energy we experience as we worship and intercede.

Praying Saints Fill in the Gap

As we worship and intercede we can be sure, that evil intentions will be found out or bound before they ever take place. We say with all of our heart and mouth, "not on our watch, not in our time," which helps preserve the coming generations. Every believer should be "making up the hedge while standing in the gap," praying and singing the Word of God effectively, and using their voice to intervene for the help of others and doing spiritual warfare as a co-laborer with God.

In conclusion, ask yourself, "When God is searching, will He find me ready and willing?" You are able through the Holy Spirit. It is a simple call. Pray. Your words are anointed by the power of God. You do your part and He will do His. But He has chosen to partner with you. He desires to do life with you not for you.

Streaming in *Heaven's Flow*

"Intercession, The Power to Intervene"

Living As His People of Prayer and Worship

I. History Belongs to the Intercessor

"Those who partner with God, to bring about His will and Kingdom on the earth, are shaping the future through prayer and intercession."

A. Intervene and Step In

Further, intercession means to "get involved, (squeeze in, get between)." This truly defines the heart of those who carry out the priestly ministry of prayer and worship.

B. Israel Pleads for an Intercessor

Numbers 21:7

*"We have sinned, because we have spoken against the LORD and you; **intercede with the LORD**, that He may remove the serpents from us,"*
*And **Moses interceded** for the people.*

II. God is Looking for Someone to Stand Up for What is Right

It is possible to ... intercede with the Lord, to intervene in the affairs of God and man.
It is possible to ... step in between, mediate, and change the outcome by righteous intercession.

A. Standing in the Gap

Every believer should be "making up the hedge while standing in the gap," praying and singing the Word of God for the help of others.

B. The New Testament Fulfillment of Ezekiel 22:30

Pray at all times (on every occasion, in every season) in the Spirit, with all [manner of] prayer and entreaty. To that end, keep alert and watch with strong purpose and perseverance, interceding in behalf of all (God's consecrated people). (AMP)

III. God's Desire is to have Many Intercessors

There is a direct connection between us praying in the will of God and the release of His justice on the earth. Prayer and intercession take deeper root in our hearts when the understanding that God makes wrong things right hits home.

A. God is Displeased that there is No Justice

Isaiah 59 : 14 - 16

> ¹⁴ **Justice** *is turned back, and righteousness stands far away; for truth has stumbled in the street, and uprightness cannot enter.*
> ¹⁵ *Yes, truth is lacking; and he who turns aside from evil makes himself a prey. Now the LORD saw, and it was displeasing in His sight that* **there was no justice***.*
> ¹⁶ *And He saw that there was* **no man***, and was astonished that there was* **no one to intercede***;*
> *Then His own arm brought salvation to Him, and His righteousness upheld Him.*

B. Beyond a Life of Ease and Comfort

Concerning prayer, this is also the truth. All it takes for evil to conquer a nation is that the Christians never pray and live a life of ease and comfort.

IV. Co-Laborers with Christ in Intercession

The mind-blowing fact is that He asks us to come join Him as co-laborers working with Him. It's self evident in I Corinthians 3:9. We are God co-workers.

A. ICorinthians 3:9

*For we are fellow workmen (***laborers together***) ***with*** and for* ***God***; *For we are God's co-workers. For we have been the helpers of God.*

B. Doing the Ministry that Jesus Does (Hebrews 7:25)

Everyone is called to pray and intercede as Jesus does with "fiery prayer and effectual power."

The Weapons of Our Spiritual Warfare

*God spent the life of
His Son to ensure that we
would have the top resources and treasuries
to draw from to do
battle with prayer and intercession.*

*As we enter into the **joy** and **labor** of
prayer and worship, we release
God's help and power into the situations.
The arms of our knighthood
are not of the flesh.
We use God's mighty weapons,
to knock down the devil's strongholds.*

Chapter Seven

The Weapons of Our Spiritual Warfare

They are Divinely Powerful Through God

2Corinthians 10:3-5

> ³ *For though we walk in the flesh, we do not **war** according to the flesh,*
>
> ⁴ *for the **weapons** of our **warfare** are not of the flesh, but divinely powerful for the destruction of fortresses.*
>
> ⁵ *We are destroying speculations and every lofty thing raised up against the knowledge of God, and we are taking every thought captive to the obedience of Christ.*

Worshippers Functioning as Prayer Warriors . . .

Worship is our fuel and prayer is our fire!

Divinely Powerful . . . are the weapons of our warfare.
Spiritual Warfare . . . is what believers do as intercessors**.**

God made sure that we would not be left defenseless or unable to pray and do His work at the highest levels. The cost of the sacrifice of the Lord Jesus on the Cross was so substantial. Our heavenly Father made sure in His overall plan that it would provide everything we need to fulfill His destiny in our lives. This plan involves us taking our place on the earth as worshipping intercessors and as those who wield the sword spiritually.

This passage of scripture is unsurpassed in its clarity and definition of spiritual warfare. It is worth extra time, study, and meditation, to capture the deeper parts of the revelation of God. Every believer, as His priests, should be actively operating in worship and intercession.

This scripture passage clearly states that:

1) Our warfare is fought in the spirit realm, not in the flesh.
2) These weapons are divinely powerful, mighty through God.
3) Our battle is stopping anything that is exalting itself against the true knowledge of God.
4) Worship, Prayer and Music are used for the destruction of spiritual strongholds.

We are warring intercessors with spiritual weapons that do spiritual warfare.

2Corinthians 10:3-5

> [3] *For though we walk in the flesh,*
> *we do not war according to the flesh,*
> *for the **weapons** of our **warfare***
> *(the arms of our knighthood) are not of the flesh,*
> *but **divinely powerful** for the destruction of fortresses,*
>
> [4] *(for the weapons of our warfare are not carnal,*
> *but **mighty through God** to the*
> ***pulling down** of strongholds).*
>
> [5] *We are destroying speculations, imaginations, and arguments and every lofty thing raised up against the knowledge of God, and we are taking every thought captive to the obedience of Christ.* (NAS, WYC, KJV, NKJV)

1) **Our Warfare** is Fought in the Spirit Realm

Not in the Flesh

2Corinthians 10:3

We are not warring after the flesh. We are fighting with His strength. It would be futile to try to use natural weapons against spiritual enemies. It's kind of a peculiar thought, but I have asked people while I am teaching, this question "if you set off a nuclear bomb next to an angel's head, guess what happens? Nothing, for angels exist and are living in another realm."

*For though we walk in the flesh, we do not **war according to** the flesh.*

*Weak men, we may be, but it is not as such that **we fight** our battles.* (NEB)

This is a major trap of the enemy to keep us fighting in the natural realm. God's strength is released in the midst of our weakness. We are not using mere human weapons, but the divine strength of the Lord of Hosts.

*For though we walk (live) in the flesh, we are not carrying on our warfare according to the flesh and **using mere human weapons**.* (AMP)

*Human indeed we are, but it is in **no human strength** that we fight our battles.* (Knox)

As we enter into worship and intercession, we move right into the middle of God's power realm. In this realm, His Kingly **authority rules**. Intercessors with this authority **overcome** from the prayer room with their prayers and intercessions. This is the realm we must dwell in to make a difference in our situations and the lives of others.

In America we spend millions and trillions of dollars for the defense of our Nation. There is no hesitation with our government and its leaders to make sure we are using our resources to protect our citizens.

In the same way, God spent the life of His Son to ensure that we would have the top resources and treasuries to draw from to do battle with prayer and intercession.

2) Our Weapons are Divinely Powerful

2 Corinthians 10:4

There is unlimited power and strength available in the Lord of Hosts. He is the God of angel armies. There are no power shortages with Him. When this dawns on everyday believers, their prayer life usually goes to another level. If we are fighting in our own strength with natural weapons, we can not last very long at that. When we are engaged with the strength of His presence and these spiritual weapons, we become a formidable force.

Zechariah 4:6 The strength and power of God

> *Then He said to me,*
> *"This is the word of the LORD to Zerubbabel saying,*
> *'Not by might (strength) nor by power, but by My Spirit,' says*
> *the LORD of hosts."* (NAS, CSB)

> *You will not succeed by your own strength or power, but by My Spirit, says the LORD All-Powerful.* (NCV)

"But by My Spirit," is in our hearts and in our mouths as we pray the Word supported by anointed music. We need to use it more often and more zealously. Darkness **is dispelled** and evil is destroyed by His power! And this power is the Holy Spirit. He is the "Enforcer" that spoils the plans of the enemy.

2 Corinthians 10:4

> *Weapons ... divinely powerful for the destruction of fortresses.*

The Lord's weapons rupture and defeat the kingdom of darkness. These weapons (worship, prayer and music) are absolutely mighty because they are before God. The was His intention from the beginning. That's why the enemy hates music and tries to use it for every evil purpose and not for the glory of God.

Isaiah 9:7 The Zeal of the Lord of Hosts

> *His (the Son of God) ruling authority will grow, and there'll be no limits to the wholeness He brings. He'll rule from the historic David throne over that promised kingdom. He'll put that kingdom on a firm footing and keep it going with fair dealing and right living, beginning now and lasting always.*

> *The zeal of **GOD**-of-the-**Angel-Armies** will do all this.*
> *God answered Fire with Fire.* (MSG)

We are being convinced by these scriptures that our spiritual weapons are divinely powerful. He is the God-of-the-

Angel-Armies according to the Message Bible. How big is our God? Almost immeasurable. Does He grow weary like the sons of men? Absolutely not! Does He sleep or slumber? He has no need for these things.

So it's in His strength
and His zeal that we can
tend the fire on the
altar of prayer and worship.

I know we can't keep up with the Lord, Himself for these bodies and voices need sleep and rest. But in our waking hours we can "Stream in Heaven's Flow" and let the mighty river of worship and intercession run at raging flood levels. We know for sure this river does two things: it brings pleasure to the heart of our Heavenly Father and torments the kingdom of darkness.

3) Our Battle is Stopping Anything Exalting Itself
against the Knowledge of God

2 Corinthians 10:5

We battle everyday and pray and intercede for the heart and mental freedom of every man. People in the world, profess themselves to be wise, and yet they become fools. For God has used the weak things of this world to confound the mighty.

The Message of the Cross is Foolishness to
Those Who are Perishing

I Corinthians 1:18-20

*18 For the story and message of the Cross is sheer absurdity and **folly** (foolishness) to those who are perishing and on their way to perdition, but to us who are being saved it is the [manifestation of] the power of God.*

19 For it is written, I will baffle and render useless and destroy the learning of the learned and the philosophy of the philosophers and the cleverness of the clever and the discernment of the discerning; I will frustrate and nullify [them] and bring [them] to nothing.

20 Where is the wise man (the philosopher)?
Where is the scribe (the scholar)?
Where is the investigator [who does] (the logistics, the debater) of this present time and age?

Has not God shown up the nonsense, the folly of this world's wisdom?

The reason we must study these scriptures is so that we can take every thought captive to the obedience of Christ. The amount of untruth that circulates on the internet alone world-wide is appalling. We must raise up the standard (flag) of truth once again concerning God's ways.

God's Foolish Things are Wiser than the Wisdom of Men

I Corinthians 1:25-27

25 [This is] because the foolish thing [that has its source in] God is wiser than men, and the weak thing [that springs] from God is stronger than men.

26 For [simply] consider your own call, brethren; not many [of you were considered to be] wise according to human estimates and standards, not many influential and powerful, not many of high and noble birth.

27 [No] for God selected (deliberately chose) what in the world is foolish to put the wise to shame, and what the world calls weak to put the strong to shame. (AMP)

Prayer has the power to
open eyes and change hearts.
It is part of the ministry of
taking every thought captive
to the Lordship of Christ.

Part of our job as intercessors is to release the Word of God, it's light and it's truth, and do it tenaciously. The amount of deceptive fantasies and philosophies world-wide is truly mind blowing.

113

The conceits of men, in their pride, gives us a whole other level of non-truth and deception. But intercession turns hearts and changes minds.

2 Corinthians 10:5

> *Our battle is to **bring down** every deceptive **fantasy** and every imposing defense that men erect against the true knowledge of God.* (Phi.)

> Yes, **we can pull down** the conceits of men and every barrier of pride which set itself up against the true knowledge of God.
> (Knox)

> *We use our powerful God-tools for **smashing warped philosophies**.* (MSG)

For the last two years, one of my prayers has been, "Lord please separate fantasy (what I think I am accomplishing spiritually but really am not) from the true reality of my daily walk with You. Point out the difference in what I am doing and the true reality of what I should be doing (Your perspective of reality)."

In my college education, I had two semesters of philosophy class. I can't begin to tell you the amount of fantasy and man-made philosophies that I heard that just reeked to high heaven. The statements were so false and so wrong I was astonished. But because I was already a Christian, a true believer in Christ, I would debate my teachers using the truth of God's Word and they grew to dislike it very much.

We need to keep our own internal thoughts from dethrone-ing Christ in our hearts. The mind is where the enemy tries to confuse us. The Holy Spirit in us guides us to all the truth. We have the ability to conquer and prevail through worship and prayer.

Back to the Weapons of Our Warfare

2 Corinthians 10:4

> *. . . for the weapons of our warfare (**arms of** our **knighthood**) are not of the flesh.* (WYC)

We use God's mighty weapons, not mere worldly weapons, to knock down the devil's strongholds. (NLT)

The weapons and tools at hand are actually referred to as the arms of our knighthood. I want to highly value the elements of our ability to do warfare in the spiritual realm. The Knights of the Roundtable were disciplined and expertly trained to use their weapons: shields and swords, bows and arrows, the war-hammer and the flail. In the same way, we are becoming more adept in wielding weapons in the spiritual realm.

*Our tools are ready at hand for **clearing** the ground of **every obstruction** and **building lives** of obedience into maturity.*
(MSG)

The Lord can take His sword in His right hand and knight us into the greater ministry of His Kingdom. Most believers will not know this anointing, until they move into the place (lifestyle) of diligent prayer. We must begin to use the tools and weapons God has provided in His spiritual arsenal. The Cross made them available to us. The veil was torn giving us full access to the Throne and all the power that dwells there.

Conquer: gaining mastery over someone or something by physical, mental, moral or spiritual force

Prevail: to gain the advantage or mastery over; be victorious; triumph by reason of greater strength / force.

Do we get it yet? We must see worship and intercession for what God intended them to be. They are working prayer tools for building and yet awesome weapons for binding the kingdom of darkness. So get busy!

4) **Worship, Prayer and Music -** Destroying Spiritual Strongholds

As we enter into the **joy** and **labor** of prayer and worship, we release God's help and power into the situations for which we pray. We have available to us weapons that release God's help and power.

Worship, Prayer and Music are working tools for building (praying, blessing, and releasing), yet powerful weapons for

115

arresting the activities of darkness (binding, stopping and destroying).

Using The Word of God with Its Full Power

The Word of God can not return void. This is why we have learned to pray and sing it in the Prayer Room. When you sing and pray the Word, it activates the stored-up power of it. I have had such great times during Prayer Room sets seeing the Word of God go forth in power. Preachers and teachers are doing the same things as they minister. But when we add music and worship to the release of the Word of God, it lasts longer and goes deeper into the hearts of those participating.

Isaiah 55:11

> *So shall My word be that goes forth out of My mouth: it shall not return to Me **void**, but it shall accomplish that which I please, and it shall **prosper** in the thing for which I sent it.* (KJV)

> *It will not return to Me **empty**, without accomplishing **what I desire**, and without succeeding in the matter for which I sent it.*
> (NAS)

Worship Itself is a Weapon

The enemies of the people of Judah and King Jehosaphat were destroyed as Judah worshipped the Living God. The power of His Presence infused in His people's praise and worship is unstoppable. King Jehosaphat sent the worshippers out **before** the army. They believed in the power of worship or they would have died.

2 Chronicles 20:21-22, 24-25

> [21] *When he (King Jehosaphat) had consulted with the people, he appointed those who **sang to the LORD** and those who **praised Him** in holy attire, as they **went out** before the army and said,*
> *"Give thanks to the LORD, for His loving-kindness is everlasting."*

> [22] *When they **began singing** and **praising**, the **LORD set ambushes** against the sons of Ammon, Moab and Mount Seir, who had come against Judah; so they were struck down*

²⁴ *When Judah came to the lookout of the wilderness, they looked toward the multitude, and behold, they were corpses lying on the ground, and **no one had escaped**.*

²⁵ *. . . Jehoshaphat and his people found much among them, goods, garments and valuable things more than they could carry. And they were three days **taking the spoil** because there was so much.*

God hasn't changed. Old Testament principles are still enforced today. Just as it was for Judah, so it is for you and me. Worship will confuse your enemies and they will destroy each other. As you can see from Psalm 8:2, the praise of children has its own power on it. This is an awesome scripture concerning the power of praise and worship. When it goes forth it can stop your enemies, revengeful tongues and even the avenger himself.

> [The avenger is the one sent out to justly carry out the sentence or punishment of a righteous judge.]

Psalm 8:2

> *Out of the mouth of babes, of infants at the breast, you have rebuked the mighty, silencing the enmity (hostility)and vengeance to teach your foes a lesson, [to cause the enemy and the **avenger** to cease].* (NEB, GLT)

> *You have taught the little children to praise You perfectly. May their example shame and silence your enemies!* (Tay.)

Thou hast made the lips of children. . .
vocal with praise,
to confound thy enemies;
to silence malicious
and revengeful tongues.
(Knox - Psalm 8:3)

[This is really verse two in other translations. It is verse three in the Knox translation because it uses the title of the Psalm as the first verse.]

Taking Up the Full Armor of God:

Staying Ready for the Battle

The full armor of God makes us properly outfitted for

prayer ministry. This is part of God's resource for entering into (doing) spiritual warfare. Be strong:

Ephesians 6:10

> *Finally, be strong in the Lord and in the strength of His might, [be **empowered through your union with Him**]; by the strength His boundless might provides.* (AMP)

> *. . . draw your strength from the Lord, the Mastery which **His conquering power** supplies.* (Con., Knox)

With well-made weapons and our armor of God, we stand against the schemes of the devil. While using invisible weapons against invisible forces we conquer and prevail. When we use the Word of God, singing or praying it out loud, it is invisible to the natural eye.

When we play anointed music from consecrated hearts, even though our worship and intercession again is invisible, it contains its own power. So it is with our worship and intercession, though invisible to the natural eye, it is a massive force.

Ephesians 6:-11

> [11] *Put on God's whole armor [the armor of **a heavy-armed soldier** which God supplies], that you may be able successfully to stand up against [all] the strategies and the deceits of the devil.* (AMP)

> [11] *So take everything the Master has set out for you, **well-made weapons** of the best materials.*

> *And **put them to use** so you will be able to stand up to everything the devil throws your way.* (MSG)

Anointed by the Holy Spirit

For years I have been singing, and playing my guitar and piano as godly weapons. I know as I am anointed by the Holy Spirit, my voice and my instruments, even in the natural, are part of my spiritual arsenal. As I am releasing the Holy Spirit through my worship and my prayer, I am fulfilling the ministry of the royal priesthood unto the Lord.

It is time for worship teams to view themselves as more than entertainment for Sunday morning. They are carriers of the presence of God who should be wielding the weapons of warfare for the advancement of the Kingdom of God and the help of His people. Worship, intercession and music are forces to be reckoned with because they are made up of the very breath we breathe. When these are joined with the presence of God, they carry the anointing that destroys every yoke.

Isaiah 10:27

> And it shall come to pass in that day, that his burden (King of Assyria) shall be taken away from off thy shoulder, and his yoke from off thy neck, and the yoke shall be **destroyed** because of the **anointing**. (KJV)

Our Fight against the Forces of Darkness

Ephesians 6:12 *For our struggle [fight] is not against flesh and blood, but . . .* (NAS, Phi.)

a) *against principalities {the rulers, despotisms, that is tyranny [ies]},*

b) *against the powers (authorities of darkness),* (NLT, YLT) *[like territorial gate keepers]*

c) *against the world forces, the various powers of evil in this darkness,* (TCNT) *against [the master spirits who are] the world rulers of this present darkness,*

d) *the spiritual forces of wickedness in high places, in supernatural sphere(s)* (KJV, AMP)

> *the spiritual agents of evil arrayed against us in the heavenly warfare.* (WNT, Phi.)

Even though all these dimensions of demonic powers and forces are mentioned in Ephesians 6, Jesus is so much more powerful. He took the abundance of our sins and the penalty for it as the Lamb of God and the Ultimate Sacrifice. He currently carries the power and the Life of the Crucified Lamb.

The scriptures record that Jesus descended into hell and met Lucifer, Satan face to face and He said, "I'll take the keys of hell and death back again." He has authority over all the realm of darkness for He reigns supreme over all the earth and even the universe itself.

Colossians 2:14-15

> [14] *having canceled out the certificate of debt consisting of decrees against us, which was hostile to us; and He has taken it out of the way, having **nailed** it to the **Cross.***

> [15] *Christ **disarmed** the principalities and powers that were ranged against us and made a bold display and public example of them, in **triumphing over** them in Him and in it [the **Cross**].* (AMP)

Let Us Forever Make the Connection

When we are doing our music, worship and intercession there is a inherent "God" power released. These three are a true form of spiritual warfare. From Colossians two, let us take heart and be relentless in our doing of an abundance of worship, passionate prayer, and fiery music.

The Power of Your Voice and Music

Isaiah 30:30-32

> [30] *And the LORD will cause **His voice of authority** to be heard, and the descending of His arm to be seen in fierce anger, and in the flame of a consuming fire in cloudburst, downpour and hailstones.*

> [31] *For at **the voice** of the LORD Assyria will be terrified, when He strikes with the rod.*

> [32] *and every blow of the rod of punishment, which the LORD will lay on him, will be **with the music** of tambourines and lyres; and in battles, brandishing weapons,*
>   ***He** will fight them.*

His energy and power in you is a weapon. You have His voice of authority in you when you are filled the Holy Spirit. You have the ability to speak and change things. That was the plan of God all along for giving you His Spirit.

That's why Jesus said in John, "But I tell you the truth, it is to your advantage that I go away; for if I do not go away, the Helper (the Holy Spirit) will not come to you; but if I go, I will send Him to you."

Use your voice. Agree with His voice by praying His Word. Words are powerful. They contain life and death according to Proverbs.

Proverbs 18: 21 and 20 (speaking/singing sacred words)

> ^{21} *Death and life are* **in the power of the tongue**, *and those who love it will eat its fruit.*
> ^{20} *With the fruit (speech) of a man's mouth his stomach will be satisfied;*
>> *He will be satisfied with the product of his lips.*

Isn't it amazing that words have power whether they are spoken or they are sung!

Anything that you can speak
can be put to melody and sung like the wind.
Anything that you are singing
can become a spoken narrative
and turned into **fervent, blazing prayer.**

The LORD, My Rock, Who Trains My Hands for War

The great King and Psalmist David in Psalm 144 leaves us a great truth concerning our final point on the weapons of our warfare. He said,

"the Lord, my Rock has trained my hands to war and my fingers for battle." This is very personal because it is God flowing through you to do His work on the earth. This is one of the highest honors a human being can ever have.

Playing music full of grace . . . He trained my hands for war

Releasing worship full of Presence . . .
in the skill of battle, my fingers flow

Speaking prayers full of faith . . .
the art of fighting, I use the Sword

Singing worship full of adoration . . .
                        my Rock, my King, my firm Strength

Psalm 144:1

*Blessed be the LORD, my rock, Who **trains** my hands*
*   for war (warfare), and my fingers for battle.* (NAS, CSB)

Blessed be the Lord, my Rock and my keen and firm Strength,
*   Who **teaches** my hands to war and my fingers to fight.*
                                                        (AMP)

*. . . teaching my hands **the use** of the sword,*
*   and my fingers **the art** of fighting.* (BBE)

*He gives me **strength** for war and **skill** for battle.* (NLT)
*He makes my hands **ready** for war, and my fingers for battle.*
                                                        (NLV)

This is one of my favorite scriptures because it is revealing that there is a spiritual warrior inside **everyone** of us.

This is a phenomenal point: I truly see the hidden value of our lives, our music and singing as they are in His hands. I have always known in my heart that music and sound have light and power on them as they are being released. Our words are powerful in the spirit realm to effect change as a type of warfare too. Even the Lord declared that He is a warrior.

Exodus 15:3

The LORD is a man of war: the LORD is His name. (KJV)
The LORD (Yahweh) is a warrior; yes, the Lord is a great soldier.
The Lord is His name. (NLT, ERV)

Come, let us join up with the abundance of the heart to be found Streaming in Heaven's Flow. Worship, prayer and music, these surely triumph over the powers of darkness. We are growing in our abilities to sing and play music that is full of the Lord's anointing.

We are deepening the lifestyle to sit at His feet and know the desires of the King of Glory's heart. Spiritual warfare has been built into the elements of worship, prayer and music. I find these thoughts super-motivating for making the long-term commitment that I will keep flowing in the priestly ministry of prayer and worship.

Oh how I love to sing. Oh how I really love to sing for Jesus. Oh how I love to play music that brings pleasure to His heart and has power to destroy the strongholds of the enemy. Our voices are singing, our hands are trained for battle and our feet are marching to Heaven's beat.

Psalm 18: 33-35

> [33] *He makes my feet like hinds' feet, and sets me upon my high places.*
> [34] *He **trains** my **hands** for battle,*
> *so that my arms can bend a bow of bronze.*
> [35] *You have also given me the shield of Your salvation and Your right hand upholds me; and Your gentleness makes me great.*

Streaming in Heaven's Flow

The Weapons of Our Spiritual Warfare

They are Divinely Powerful Through God

I. Worshippers Functioning as Prayer Warriors

God made sure that we would not be left defenseless or unable to pray and do His work at the highest levels. The cost of the sacrifice of the Lord Jesus on the Cross was so substantial.

A. Divinely Powerful . . . are the weapons of our warfare.

1) Our warfare is fought in the spirit realm, not in the flesh.

2) These weapons are divinely powerful, mighty through God.

3) Our battle is stopping anything that is exalting itself against the true knowledge of God.

4) Worship, Prayer and Music are used for the destruction of spiritual strongholds.

B. Using The Word of God with Its Full Power

The Word of God can not return void. *It will not return to Me **empty**, without accomplishing **what I desire**, and without succeeding in the matter for which I sent it.* (NAS)

II. Worship Itself is a Weapon

There is unlimited power and strength available in the Lord of Hosts. He is the God of angel armies. There are no power shortages with Him. When this dawns on everyday believers, their prayer life usually goes to another level.

A. *"Not by might (strength) nor by power, but by My Spirit, says the LORD of hosts."* (NAS, CSB)

B. Darkness **is dispelled** and evil is destroyed by His power! And this power is the Holy Spirit. He is the "enforcer" that spoils the plans of the enemy.

*We use our powerful God-tools for **smashing warped philosophies**.* (MSG)

III. Taking Up the Full Armor of God

The full armor of God makes us properly outfitted for prayer ministry. This is part of God's resource for entering into (doing) spiritual warfare.

A. When we play anointed music even though our worship and intercession is invisible to the natural eye, it contains its own power. Our worship and intercession is a commanding force.

IV. Anointed by the Holy Spirit

A. Worship, intercession and music have spiritual force.

1) They are made up of the very breath we breathe.

2) When these are joined with the presence of God, they carry the anointing that destroys every yoke.

B. Worship teams are carriers of the presence of God and should be wielding the weapons of godly warfare,

1) for the advancement of the Kingdom of God

2) and the help of His people.

V. Our Fight against the Forces of Darkness

A. Because of His sacrifice, Jesus has all authority. He sits on the Throne as the Victorious Lion and the Crucified Lamb.

This is why we can fight with Christ
*against principalities {the rulers of tyrannies . . .
against the powers (authorities of darkness),* (NLT, YLT)
*   [like territorial gate keepers] . . .
the world rulers of this present darkness, the spiritual forces
of wickedness in high places, in supernatural sphere(s)*
(KJV, AMP)

Colossians 2:15

*Christ **disarmed** the principalities and powers that were ranged against us and made a bold display and public example of them, in **triumphing over** them in Him and in it [the **Cross**].* (AMP)

Let's be relentless in our doing of an abundance of worship, passionate prayer, and fiery music

Singing and Praying the Word of God

*The Living Word set to music,
sung from hearts on fire,
it's a pure, righteous spiritual force!*

*As we sing and pray
the Word of God with all of our heart,
it releases the stored-up power
that is in the Word of God.
Our hearts create spontaneous melodies
and our minds form lyrics that become
holy songs of praise.
These are songs that are generated,
on the spot, by the Holy Spirit in you.*

Chapter Eight

Singing and Praying the Word of God

His Word Will Not Return Void or Empty

Isaiah 55:11

*So will **My Word** be which goes forth from My mouth;*
*It will not return to Me **empty** (void), without accomplishing what I desire,*
and without succeeding in the matter for which I sent it.

*So is My word it **turns not** back unto Me empty, but has done that which I desired, and prosperously **effected** that [for] which I sent it.* (YLT)

*It is the same with my word. I send it out, and it **always produces fruit**.*
It will accomplish all I want it to, it will prosper everywhere I send it. (NLT)

Learning the Bible by Singing Scripture Choruses

In the 1970's and 80's, we learned the Bible by singing Scripture choruses. There is probably no other way we would have known so much of the Bible without the power of singing the Word of God. Thousands of people from non-Bible reading backgrounds came into the greater depths of the Word because the Word was set to music.

In the same way today, the Scriptures are finding their way back into our church songs, our modern choruses and is a large part our time in the Prayer Room. We are so much stronger spiritually because we are singing and praying the Word of God.

People in third world countries have no problem doing this as long as they have Bibles in their possession. Singing and praying the Word of God is not based on having a high level education, financial status or social skills. It's based on their love for God, their hunger for the help of the Lord and their heart to see God's kingdom established in their region and city.

Psalms, Hymns and Spiritual Songs

This is the pattern now for the New Testament believers. I am sure that I would have never lasted in the pattern of Old Testament law and worship. Just imagine if you had to kill a bull or a goat and collect its blood and offer it as a sacrifice. I am not trying to gross you out but I want you to give thanks that Jesus shed His blood one time for you that you might have a new and living way into the presence of God.

Colossians 3:16

> Let the **word of Christ** *(our Lord) richly dwell within you, with all wisdom teaching and admonishing one another with*
>
> ***psalms,*** *(a song composed on a divine subject, in praise of God)*
>
> ***hymns,*** *(a song, an ode or a poem in honor of God put to music)*
>
> ***spiritual songs,*** *(songs generated from the hearts of believers touched by the power of the Holy Spirit)*
>
> *singing with thankfulness in your hearts to God.*
>
> *Let the teaching of Christ and His words keep on **living in you**. Keep on teaching and helping each other.*
> *Sing the **Songs of David** and*
> *the **church songs** and*
> *the **songs of Heaven** with hearts full of thanks to God.* (NLV)

150 Psalms for Singing Until Jesus Comes Back Again!

This so important for all of us to understand. There are 150 songs which are now 150 Psalms canonized in our Bible. People have been singing these for over 3,000 years. They have

every aspect of life, up and down, telling about of the condition of the heart of man on their worst days and their best days.
[Here's what Matthew Henry's Commentary says about the Psalms:

The singing of psalms is
a **teaching** ordinance
as well as a **praising** ordinance.
We are not only to quicken
and encourage ourselves,
but to *teach and admonish one another,*
mutually excite our **affections**,
and convey instructions.

When we sing psalms, we make no melody unless we sing with grace in our hearts, (because) we are suitably affected by what we sing. We go along in it with true devotion and understanding.

So, we **must** *admonish one another in psalms and hymns (and spiritual songs).* Observe, singing of psalms is a gospel ordinance. (They were) suited to special occasions, instead of their lewd and profane songs in their idolatrous worship.]

The Treasury of David

Years ago, a great man of God wrote a book called "The Treasury of David." His name was Charles Haddon Spurgeon (1834-1892). He was born in Essex, England. Of all his writings, the one that is his greatest work is "The Treasury of David," composed and polished over the span of nearly half his ministry. He first published this treasury in weekly installments over a twenty-year span in the London Metropolitan Tabernacle's periodical, The Sword and the Trowel.

Within a decade more than 120,000 sets had been sold. The Treasury of David is a superb literary achievement. Eric Hayden, pastor of the Metropolitan Tabernacle a century after Spurgeon's ministry began there, calls this work "Spurgeon's magnum opus." Spurgeon's wife said that if Spurgeon had never written any other work, this would have been a permanent literary memorial. (Studylight.org)

Most people understand the definition of what hymns are and how they function. It is a very rich tradition that has been carried on through the church and the people of God. This brings us to understanding the meaning of spiritual songs.

Breaking Out in Spiritual Songs

Spiritual songs are songs generated from the hearts of believers who are touched by the power of the Holy Spirit. This is one of the coolest forms of singing and music ever. It releases a singer from singing a fully written out set of lyrics to a prewritten melody.

This is some of the most enjoyable singing a singer can ever do on the earth. It's like creating art on the fly. It's like a toddler doing finger painting. The song and the lyrics are created from the spiritual flow, the energy and the emotion of the moment the singer is singing in.

The same is true for musicians. In place of lyrics, they are playing a river of music notes over chord progressions that are free flowing from their hands and their heart. It is so very freeing and the sense of fulfillment is most times overwhelming.

Spiritual Songs in the Prayer Room

The use of spiritual songs in the Prayer Room is one of our greatest foundational tools. I know there are people reading this book right now that are freaking out and semi-withdrawing from this concept. But singers regardless of their training, can adapt to this natural well of creativity that is within them.

So when the opportunity arises, give it your best shot. You can start by doing training sessions that help people match their melodies to the chord progression that is being played. Little by little, you will become more comfortable with doing it and actually become very proficient at it.

Ephesians 5:19

> But **drink deeply** of God's Spirit. **Speak out** to one another in psalms and hymns and spiritual songs,
>
> offering praise with voices [and instruments] and making melody with all your heart to the Lord,

joining with one another
    *in **holy songs** of praise and **of the Spirit**,*
***using your voice** in songs and making melody*
    in your heart to the Lord. (BBE)

*... singing, and **striking the strings**, with your heart*
    unto the Lord. (REB)

I want to point out these two categories from Ephesians 5. The first is holy songs of praise and the second is holy songs of the Spirit. This is really important because so many singers and musicians have been trained only in performance based music and singing. Their tendency is to do exactly what is set before them on the music sheet.

These two categories give us the freedom to venture out to sing more from our hearts than from our minds. It's found and accessed much more in the presence based orientation. The anchor point is the same for all of us.

We are singing and praying the Word of God with all of our heart engaged. All while our minds are creating spontaneous melodies and lyrics. It's truly making use of this type of singing called holy songs of praise, songs and music that are generated by the Holy Spirit.

Singing and praying the Word is a necessary stream and part of any Prayer Room. As your church singers and musicians learn how to do this, three powerful things begin to happen:

- ❖ First, they are **releasing** the power of God's Word in a consistent and long-term manner.

- ❖ Second, they are using the Word of God to **bind up** principalities and powers in the kingdom of darkness.

- ❖ Third, they are learning, memorizing and getting the Scripture **deep** in their **hearts**.

" I Will Sing of Your Word" - Singing the Scriptures

The Word of God plays an integral part in worship and prayer. The Hebrew understanding of singing and praying the

Word comes from the tradition of how they sing and pray the Torah (the books of Moses, the first five books of our Bible).

Today the Jewish people are still singing and praying the Torah on the Western Wailing Wall in Jerusalem. At modern Synagogue services today, there is a **cantor** who sings and prays the Word leading the people to do the same. He is singing lines from Scriptural prayers of the Torah.

Psalm 119:171–172

> [171] *Let my lips **utter praise**, for You teach me Your statutes.*

> [172] *Let my tongue **sing of Your Word**, for all Your command-ments are righteousness (justice). My tongue does sing of Thy saying(s), for all Thy commands [are] righteous.* (YLT)

> *My tongue shall sing [praise for the **fulfillment**] of Your word, for all Your commandments are righteous.* (AMP)

> *And let your promises **ring** from my tongue;* (MSG)
> *Let me sing about your promises;* (NCV)

Sing of Your Word - [ʾanah] - to sing . . . utter tunefully . . . melodious : having a pleasant melody

The primary meaning is to sing, hence to cry out our singing or cantor.

A focused effort to learn how to flow with worship into intercession will benefit everybody. Integrating the Word of God into our worship and prayer is super important because of its value and power.

God's People Singing and Praying the Bible

God's people singing and praying the Bible is a powerful force for the greater release of His Word, with His Light and Power on it. It is "Streaming in Heaven's Flow" of mercy, grace and justice and . . . faith.

Romans 10 : 17

> *Faith comes by **hearing**, and **hearing** by the Word of God.*

This is the salvation message found in the Book of Romans. We hear the Gospel, we have faith and believe in Jesus, and we are saved. It's all right here.

Romans 10:13, 15-17

> ¹³ *for "WHOEVER WILL CALL ON THE NAME OF THE LORD WILL BE SAVED."*

> ¹⁵ ... *"HOW BEAUTIFUL ARE THE FEET OF THOSE WHO **BRING GOOD NEWS** OF GOOD THINGS!"*

> ¹⁶ *However, they did not all heed the good news [the gospel]; for Isaiah says, "LORD, WHO HAS BELIEVED OUR REPORT?"*

> ¹⁷ *So **faith** comes from **hearing**, and*
>   * **hearing** by the **word of Christ**.*

Luke 8:11

> *"Now the parable is this: **the seed** is the Word of God."*

I Peter 1:23

> *For you have been born again not of seed which is perishable but imperishable, that is, through the **living** and **enduring** Word of God.*

The fact that the Word of God is the seed, should be most important to us. When we are singing and praying the Word, we are planting seeds of life, seeds of beauty and seeds of righteousness in the power of His glory.

Who would not want to be part of a ministry that is doing this? See, there is an everyday-ness to be learned about doing praise with prayer, intercession with powerful music. Once you get it, you never want to stop doing it.

When these "Word of God" seeds are planted, they will always germinate because they are full of the Life of God. This is why prayer and intercession combined with deep worship and anointed music should be flowing in every section of the earth. Just to make it very clear, this is **imperishable seed** that is the living and enduring Word of God that brings great results.

The Living Word

What is it that keeps us from dedicated study of the Bible? Why is it that so many other things are so important that they take priority over knowing the Word of God?

We must begin to make good proof of not only the value of the Word of God but the power that is released in it when we read it. When we mediate on it, when we study it and when we actually put the Word of God to use, it proves itself.

The Living Word set to music, sung from hearts on fire, it's a pure, righteous spiritual force!!

We Are Too Distracted, Too at Ease

Why did we ever stop singing the Word of God? When was it that we let the importance of the Word of God slip from our hearts and minds? We will definitively rule and reign and operate with the Word of God over in eternity.

We have become too distracted and too comfortable and at ease. It is neutralizing our spiritual hunger and thirst. We have had too much of so many good things for so long that we have deceived our own heart by being "not doers of the Word."

Doers of the Word of God, not Hearers Only

James1:22-25

> [22] But prove yourselves **doers** of the word, and not merely hearers who **delude** themselves.
>
> [23] For if anyone is a hearer of the word and not a doer, he is like a man who looks at his natural face in a mirror;
>
> [24] for once he has looked at himself and gone away, he has immediately forgotten what kind of person he was.
>
> [25] But one who looks intently at the perfect law, the law of liberty, and abides by it, not having become a **forgetful hearer** but an **effectual doer**, this man will be blessed in what he does.

This scripture clearly states that we deceive our own hearts when we hear the Word only and do not do it or activate it in our lives. So this brings us to the importance of singing and praying the Word of God on top of anointed music.

The height of prayer and intercession that can be reached when it is birthed out of pure, deep worship is phenomenal. This is where the soul and the spirit have become one. Also, our total focus is on the Lord Himself. Out of this focus without any interruption we can do prayer, intercession and spiritual warfare at very high levels. This kind of spiritual warfare is stronger because it's covered by His holy presence as it is being released in our lives.

Worship, Prayer and Music at Work Together

A focused effort to learn how to flow with worship into intercession will benefit everybody. Integrating the Word of God into our worship and prayer is super important because of its value and power. The hidden treasure of the Bible is the reason that singing and praying the Word is counted as a necessary stream of any Prayer Room or prayer movement.

Anything spoken can be sung, or uttered tunefully. Our words can be sung to spontaneous, pleasant melodies. These words and melodies arise together, flowing from our hearts in those anointed moments. They are built to run together.

Words that we sing and put to music
will be remembered longer
and inscribed deeper
into our hearts and minds.
The very nature of singing
and music causes this to happen.

God's Word prayed out loud, while singers echo His Word in song is powerful. All of this activity supported by anointed music and worship is an unstoppable force. It literally **activates the Word** which will not return void.

It is time to **refocus** on the very Book that the Lord left in our hands to be able to finish our prophetic journey. The Word helps us fulfill this awesome destiny He has given to each and every one. The power of the Word, the Light of the Word, the Holy Spirit revealing the Word of God is equipping us to do spiritual work. By its revelation, there can be no mistaking where we should be going and what we should be doing with our lives.

Jump into the Realm of Doing Worship, Prayer and Music

When the people of God begin to sing and pray the Scriptures, it releases the **stored-up power** that is in the Word of God. I am thoroughly convinced that any person who knows Jesus and understands their salvation would immediately want to jump into the realm of worship, prayer and music; especially when they know the ramifications of their actions and activities.

This is why Streaming in Heaven's Flow has such meaning and power on it. If we see a model from Heaven's realm, and it is full of anointing and bearing fruit, how much more should we enter into the same actions. The Word of God will endure forever.

Isaiah 40:8

> *The grass is withered, and the flower is fallen: but the word of our Lord **endures for ever**.* (RHE)

> *"The grass withers, the flowers fade, but the word of our God **remains** forever."* (CSB)

> *"Grass dies and wildflowers fall. But the word of our God **continues** forever."* (ERV)

> *The grass, hath withered, The flower, hath faded, - But the word of our God, shall stand unto times age-abiding!* (REB)

> *The grass withers,*
> *and the flower fades,*
> *but the word of our Lord,*
> *it endures forever,*
> *it remains forever,*
> *it continues forever.*

As this power in the Word of God comes forth [singing it and praying it] it now becomes **transforming power** that

136

changes the spiritual atmosphere and the condition of our hearts.

Any time we get together, singing and playing around the Word of God, faith will start growing and rising. This is why even rehearsals should be partially built around doing real worship. Before or after learning new songs, spend time in prayer that builds the heart flow of every team member.

The Word of God is Living, Active, and Full of Power

Another giant point is that the Word of God is living and active. So many words we say everyday go unfulfilled or die out because our words have very little power on them. God's Word is not that way.

People make promises with their words that they never keep. People make up stories with their words that are lies or fabrications of the current situation. There are millions of words spoken into the atmosphere all over the world everyday.

Hebrews 4:12

For the word of God is

living and *active* and *sharper*
than any two-edged sword, and

piercing as far as the division of soul and spirit,
of both joints and marrow,

able to *judge* the *thoughts* and *intentions* of the heart.

For the **Word of God speaks,**

it is *alive* and full of *power* [making it
active, operative, energizing, and effective];

it is *sharper* than any two-edged sword,

penetrating to the dividing line
of the breath of life (soul) and [the immortal] spirit,
and of joints and marrow
[of the deepest parts of our nature],

exposing, *sifting,* analyzing and judging
the very thoughts and *purposes* of the heart. (AMP)

But when we pick up God's Word, when we sing God's Word, when we pray God's Word, it is another level. The Word of

137

God produces fruit and very sure results. The Lord keeps His Word for His Word has power and He backs up His promises.

The Heart and Ability of God's Word

Isaiah 55:11

> So will **My Word** be which goes forth from My mouth;
>
> It will not return to Me **empty** (void or unfulfilled),
>   without accomplishing what I desire, what I **intend**,
>   and without succeeding in the matter for which I sent it.
>
> So is My word it turns not back unto Me empty,
> but has done that which **I desired**, and prosperously
>   **effected** that [for] which **I sent it**.   (YLT,)
>
> It is the same with My word. I send it out,
> and it **always produces fruit**. It will accomplish
>   all I want it to, it will prosper everywhere I send it.
> (NLT, CJB, AMP)

I believe that there has been a great fight in the hearts and minds of Christians on how far you can really take the Word of God. How much can you believe in the Bible before seemingly you have lost your common sense and people feel that you have become cultic with it? The Holy Spirit would never lead you astray like that. He has come to lead you and guide you in all the truth.

The Word of God is piercing.
It is for blessing and binding
in prayer and intercession.

We must not under value it,
and learn the "every-day-ness"
of using it in prayer and worship.

Really the Word of God was given to us for many reasons. It is not the word of a man. It is not that the word of a co-worker or a neighbor. **Do We Get It Yet?** It is the Word of the Living God. If we pick up the Word of God, singing and praying it, there are great results that will happen. I will never grow weary of singing and praying the Word of God. The fact that we will be using the Word of God in eternity should encourage us to do it more now.

The Word of God Waters and Causes Growth

Isaiah 55:10 This verse gives us the reference point for the real power of God's Word we saw in verse 11.

For as the rain and the snow come down from heaven, and do not return there

*without **watering** the earth and **making** it bear and sprout, and **furnishing** seed to the sower and bread to the eater;*

... but soak the earth, and water it, and make it to spring, and give seed to the sower, and bread to the eater. (RHE)

I am so sorry that I did not pay more attention to studying and doing of the Word of God when I had the chance. In 2009, I found myself praying in the Prayer Room, "Lord, restore the time that I should have paid more attention to Your Word and I did not. I was gliding, I was just living off the strong worship gift and the anointing of Your presence."

This happened, partly because the worship meetings were going good and there was no sense of urgency to study the Word. What a mistake!

In the last four years, I believe the Lord has answered my prayer. I never read a Bible until I was nineteen years old. I was raised in the Catholic Church. There was little emphasis at that time on the personal reading of the Bible.

In the first five years of my salvation, I was totally consumed with it. My friends and I were staying in the Word of God hours a day. We visited old and rare bookstores for Bibles and Christian resource books. We knew these books could help us deepen our understanding and revelation of the Word of God. This is one of the reasons why, I will never ever stop singing and praying the Word of God.

Streaming *in* Heaven's Flow

Singing and Praying the Word of God

His Word Will Not Return Void or Empty

Today, the Scriptures are finding their way back into our church songs, our modern choruses and is a large part our time in the Prayer Room. We are so much stronger spiritually because we are singing and praying the Word of God.

I. Psalms, Hymns and Spiritual Songs

A. Let the **Word of Christ** (our Lord) richly dwell within you.

Let the teaching of Christ and **His words keep on living in you.**

B. Psalm - a song composed on a divine subject, in praise of God. Sing the Songs of David. There are 150 Psalms available for singing and praying.

The singing of psalms is a teaching ordinance as well as a praising ordinance. We are not only to quicken and encourage ourselves, but teach and admonish one another.

Let's resource the book, "The Treasury of David" by Charles Spurgeon and mine the gems that are in it.

C. Hymn - a song, an ode or a poem in honor of God put to music. Keep singing the church (Gospel) songs.

D. Spiritual Songs - songs of the moment, spontaneous songs, and the songs of Heaven.

These are songs generated from the hearts of believers touched by the power of the Holy Spirit.

The use of spiritual songs in the Prayer Room is one of our greatest foundational tools.

Ephesians 5:19- *drink deeply of God's Spirit. Speak out to one another in psalms and hymns and spiritual songs, joining with one another in holy songs of praise and of the Spirit.*

II. "I Will Sing of Your Word" - Singing the Scriptures

Sing of Your Word - ['anah] - to sing . . . utter tunefully . . . melodious : having a pleasant melody.

A. God's People Singing and Praying the Bible

It is through the living and enduring Word of God that we have all that we have anyway. Jesus upholds all things by the word of His power. It just makes sense that we would invest time in singing and praying it.

B. A focused effort to learn how to flow with worship into intercession will benefit everybody. Integrating the Word of God into our worship and prayer is super important because of its value and power.

C. When "Word of God" seeds are planted, they will always germinate because they are full of the Life of God. Prayer and intercession combined with anointed music should be flowing in every section of the earth. This imperishable seed is the Word of God that brings great results.

III. Worship, Prayer and Music at Work Together

A. The hidden treasure of the Bible is the reason that singing and praying the Word is counted as a necessary stream of any Prayer Room or prayer movement.

B. Words that we sing and put to music will be remembered longer and inscribed deeper into our hearts and minds. The nature of singing and music causes this to happen.

C. God's Word prayed out loud, while singers echo His Word in song is powerful. This activity supported by anointed music and worship is an unstoppable force. It literally activates the Word which will not return void.

IV. The Word of God is Living, Active, and Full of Power

A. The Heart and Ability of God's Word

Isaiah 55:11- *So will **My Word** be which goes forth from My mouth; It will not return to Me **empty** (void or unfulfilled), without accomplishing what I desire, what I **intend**, and without succeeding in the matter for which I sent it.*

B. The Word of God is piercing. It is for blessing and binding in prayer and intercession. We must not under value it, and learn the "every-day-ness" of using it in prayer and worship.

The High Praises of God
and
The Two-Edged Sword

*Let the high praises of God
be in your mouth,
and then, in a holy zeal for His honor,
take a two-edged sword in your hand,
and fight His battles against
the enemies of His kingdom.*

*When we are doing our music, worship
and intercession there is a inherent
"God" power released in it. It is a true form of
spiritual warfare. It blesses and helps
real people while thwarting
the activities of the kingdom of darkness.*

Chapter Nine

The High Praises of God
in Our Mouth

The Two-Edged Sword
in Our Hand

This is the honor for all His Godly Ones:
The power of worship and prayer
releases justice and judgment.

Psalm 149:5-9

[5] *Let the godly ones exalt in glory;*
*let them **sing** for joy **on** their **beds**.*
[6] *Let the **high praises** of God be in their mouth,*
*and a **two-edged sword** in their hand,*
[7] *To execute vengeance on the nations,*
and punishment on the peoples.
[8] *To bind their kings with chains,*
and their nobles with fetters of iron,
[9] *To execute on them **the judgment** written;*
***this is an honor** for all His godly ones. Praise the LORD!*

It begins for me with the power of a human voice to utter words that ride on wonderful melodies. These melodies and words affect both the hearer and the spiritual realm into which they are released. We have so much music and so many songs flooding by us in our average day that we have grown used to the impact of even the simplest song.

When you go back through human history . . .

You find the simplest songs are
life changing, load bearing
and have the power to carry
the human soul
through the darkest of hours.

In my junior year of college at Webster University in St. Louis, we were half way through our second semester in Music History. When I opened my book, to chapter 14, the title said, "Negro Spirituals." I was so impacted by this title. I had been exposed to Negro Spirituals through the ministry of praise and worship I was doing.

There was a whole chapter in my music history book dedicated to some of the simplest songs ever created accompanied by uncomplicated singing. These songs carried the African slaves through the length and breadth of one of the darkest hours of human history. Even in the midst of their awful circumstances and situations in America, they kept singing.

[As Negro Spirituals are Christian songs, most of them concern what the Bible says and how to live with (in) the Spirit of God. For example, the "dark days of bondage" were enlightened by the hope and faith that God will not leave the slaves alone.]

(NegroSpirituals.com)

The High Praises of God

To the point, the high praises of God were simple songs that the Hebrew people sang. They are full of what we now know as the canonized Word of God. Simple word phrases were put to simple melodies and used for powerful worship to the Living God.

[canonized: an authoritative list of books accepted as Holy Scripture

(Webster)]

So the tradition of simple, spontaneous songs now carries through. In the late 1960's, Jesus People took the book of Psalms and put it to simple music to sing about their Jesus. Then in my life in the 1970's and 80's, we sang scripture songs and choruses put to modern music.

People seeking the Lord
in that era (1970's and 80's)
actually learned
the Word of God
by singing Scripture songs.

New believers who had never cracked open a Bible before, learned the Word of God because it was put to melody in a song with music. People from denominational backgrounds (Charismatic Renewal) also learned the Word of God more in depth because they too were singing these scripture songs. It was a worship, song movement that went around the world in less than 20 years.

The tradition carries on today. We are using the high praises of God and the two-edged sword in our Prayer Room at Destiny Church. Focused prayer riding on top of the zeal of worship is unstoppable. The combining (intermingling) of praise with prayer and worship with intercession includes the Word of God prayed and sung. This is the true definition of using the high praises of God and the Word of God as a two-edged sword.

I have one more thought on my study of Negro Spirituals and it is this.

[In the early nineteenth century, African Americans were involved in the "Second Awakening." They met in camp meetings and sang without any hymnbook. **Spontaneous songs were composed on the spot**. They were called "spiritual songs" and the term "sperichil" (spiritual) appeared for the first time in the book "Slave Songs of The United States."] (by Allen, Ware, Garrison, 1867)

Spontaneous Songs and Songs of the Moment

Songs in worship created on the spot while flowing in His presence has been a large part of my life from the very beginning of my worship leading. I started leading worship in 1974 in my youth group. In the very beginning, we had waves of worship and the presence of God came through our meetings.

I have always viewed it as the grace of God that would help us plumb the depths of deeper worship. The Lord was modeling "Streaming in Heaven's Flow" for us. These were multiple experiences in the Holy Spirit that helped us sustain a life of prayer and worship.

Here are a few dimensions of the high praises of God as I see it.

- ❖ Everyone has a choice: by your will to enter in to the Stream of God or to not enter in.
- ❖ There is an understanding that songs and music are a large part of doing high praises. We use music as one of the weapons in our arsenal.
- ❖ All the singers and musicians are open to flowing in the Holy Spirit and operating in the presence of God as our base and foundation.

The singing of Scripture songs has started rising again today. Now in the 21st century, worship, prayer and music are spreading faster because of the internet. A song can go around the world in 48 hours.

High Praises of God and a Two-Edged Sword in Our Hands

The high songs of GOD be in their throat. .
and a sword that cuts both ways (REB, NLV)

The following quote comes from the Matthew Henry. It sums up verse six of Psalm 149 in very powerful way.

Let the high praises of God
be in their mouth,
and then, in a holy zeal for His honor,
let them take a *two-edged sword*
in their hand,
to fight His battles against
the enemies of His kingdom.

These (high praises of God) began in Moses and Joshua, who, when they taught Israel *the high praises of the Lord,* did put *a two-edged sword in their hand.*

146

David did so too, for, as he was the sweet singer of Israel, (Psalmist) so he was the captain of their hosts. (He) taught the children of Judah the use of the bow and taught their hands to war, as God had taught his.   (Matthew Henry Commentary, Psalm 149)

Verse one of Psalm 144 goes hand in hand with verse six of Psalm 149. They both speak of the warfare theme and of what God has put in our hands. I have always viewed my voice, my guitar, my hands and my piano as extensions of my life and heart. Further, I see them as consecrated, dedicated weapons made ready for God's use.

Psalm 144:1-2

> [1] *Blessed be the LORD, my rock,*
> *Who trains my hands for war, and my fingers for battle;*

> [2] *My lovingkindness and my fortress, my stronghold and*
> *my deliverer, my shield and He in whom I take refuge,*
> *Who subdues my people under me.*

> [1] *Bless the LORD, who is my rock.*
> *He gives me strength for war and skill for battle* (NLT)

> [2] *He's the bedrock on which I stand,*
> *the castle in which I live, my rescuing knight,*
> *The high crag where I run for dear life,*
> *while he lays my enemies low.*   (MSG)

Let Us Forever Make The Connection

Matthew Henry makes some really strong points on Psalm 149. "*Let the high praises of God be in their mouth,* "and then, in a holy zeal for His honor.

I want to make this point about **holy zeal** for the **Lord's honor**. As long as we continue to be outer court believers that do not know Him intimately, it will be hard to dial up the fire to use praise and worship as a tool in the church and a weapon against the kingdom of darkness. The more that we commit our time and energy to worship, prayer and music, our times of encountering God will grow and expand.

With all of my heart, I want to live in this holy zeal for the Lord's honor. Every time I lead worship and every time that I pray

His honor is the baseline for what I am doing. Simply because of His great sacrifice and glory, He deserves our best voice, our best songs, our best energy and our best attention.

The last part of the Matthew Henry quote, says this:

" . . . let them take a *two-edged sword in their hand,* **to fight** His battles against **the enemies** of His kingdom."

Now we are talking about our place to serve the Lord at the highest level. The fact that we can partner with God on anything is a profound blessing. We can do the ministry that Jesus is doing, Hebrews 7:25 - He ever lives to make intercession. The Lord Jesus also asked us to be co-laborers with Him in walking out the purposes and missions of the Father's heart.

Your Worship, Your Singing and Your Music

So there is something to be done in helping to fight His battles against the enemies of His Kingdom. I find this so arresting that any of my singing, worship and music could actually affect change concerning the kingdom of darkness.

It is one of the chief reasons that I wrote this book. Behold His majesty. Fall on your face and adore Him. Spend 20 minutes worshipping at His feet. Then arise with your voice, your musical instrument and your full heart to help fight the enemies of His Kingdom.

When we are doing our music, worship and intercession, there is a inherent "God power" released in it that is a true form of spiritual warfare. It blesses and helps real people while thwarting the activities of the kingdom of darkness.

Psalm 149:6-9

> [6] *Let the **high praises** of God be in their mouth,*
> *and a **two-edged sword** in their hand,*
> [7] *To execute vengeance on the nations,*
> *and punishment on the peoples.*
> [8] *To bind their kings with chains,*
> *and their nobles with fetters of iron,*
>
> [9] *To execute on them **the judgment** written;*
> ***this is an honor** for all His godly ones. Praise the LORD!*

Operating in the Spiritual Realm

The power of God is released in high praises and deep worship. The Sword of the Spirit is the Word of God with all of His life in it. As battle was once done in the natural, we can now do battle in spiritual warfare through music and intercession. The weapons of our warfare are not carnal and we use them against demonic strongholds and principalities:

- ❖ to execute vengeance against dark authorities
- ❖ chastisement on the forces of wickedness,
- ❖ binding principalities and powers
- ❖ executing on them the **judgment written!**

I want you to understand that this
"honor for all of His godly ones" (verse 9)
is in using
"the high praises of God and
the two-edged sword"
to do battle against the enemies of God.

It maybe a new concept for you but it has been time proven through the ages. This process has power on it. As you look at the next few pages, you will make a clear connection between doing worship and intercession and seeing the justice and judgments of God unleashed.

Measuring out the Justice and Judgment of God

Jesus said, . . ."The ruler of this world has been **judged**."

John 16:7-11

[7] *But I tell you the truth, it is to your advantage that I go away; for if I do not go away, the **Helper** will not come to you; but if I go, I will send Him to you.*
[8] *And He, when He comes, will convict the world concerning sin and righteousness and **judgment**;*
[9] *concerning sin, because they do not believe in Me; and*

¹⁰ *concerning righteousness,*
    because I go to the Father and you no longer see Me; and

¹¹ *concerning **judgment,***
    *because **the ruler** of this world **has been judged**.*

We have a role with our prayers, music and intercessions to help release the judgments that have already been written by the Lord Himself against the kingdom of darkness. There is some of God's power and light released while we are doing prayer and worship.

We give **all** the **glory** to the Lord, we know it is generated by the power of His Holy Spirit. We approach these things with all humility but we take our place as **warring worshippers**.

We must take advantage of the years that the Lord gives us. As we continue in the Prayer Room, we will have long lasting results stepping in between good and evil and the affairs of God and man.

When we are singing and praying the Word of God, the written Word is judgment in and of itself enough to overpower evil and triumph over darkness.

This is why our time in worship and intercession plays such a vital role. The real truth of the matter is that most American believers have not studied or understood the realm of the justice and judgment of God. It's gotten to the place that God is just all loving and there is really no judgment in the end. And I say, poppycock!

If this offends you, I strongly recommend you begin a Bible study to learn about who He really is and how He operates. Ask Him to reveal the realm of His holiness to you. Some of this will be shocking because He is much more than you currently know and have estimated Him to be.

Worshipping Intercessors in His Army

John 12:31-32

> [31]"*Now **judgment** is upon this world; now the ruler of this world will be cast out.*
> [32] *And I, if I am lifted up from the earth, will draw all men to Myself."*

We, as the servants of the Lord, stand as worshipping intercessors in His Army. As we pray the Word of God, we release the stored up, transforming power of His Word. Along with this is the release of His justice and judgment. When we intercede, we become "a **mouthpiece** of the Lord" on the earth doing His bidding and the "judgments written" are being released and enforced.

We have been raised up like Queen Esther for **such a time as this**: to sing and pray out the judgments and justice of God on the earth as worshipping intercessors. For like Esther, we are here to help save cities and nations and abandoned people groups all over the earth.

God's Intention in Releasing His Presence: For Our Help

Our help is His Presence. His Word is given as our help. Now I know my help comes from the Lord. My help comes from His **Presence**. . . His **Name** . . . and from His very **Being**.

Psalm 121:1-2

> [1] *I will lift my eyes up to the hills [around Jerusalem, to sacred Mount Zion and Mount Moriah] from where shall my help come?* (AMP)

> [2] ***My help comes from the LORD,***
> > *Maker of the heaven and the earth.* (GLT)

> *My help comes from **ADONAI** . . . from the **Master Lord**, Who has rulership and dominion over heaven and earth.*
> > (CJB, Lex.)

> *No, my strength comes from GOD, who made heaven, and earth, and mountains.* (MSG)

Adonai is another name used for God in the Old Testament. It is the plural form of Adon which means "Master" or "Lord." It conveys the idea of rulership or dominion.

(Blue Letter Bible Lexicon FAQ)

Our take away of this name "Adonai" literally means that the LORD is the Master of all spirits. It covers all spirits whether good or evil. [i.e. angels or angelic spirits, demons or demonic spirits, humans or human spirits].

This is the huge reason why people who believe in Jesus do not have to live in fear of the spirit realm because He is the Master of all spirits. (Psalm 121:2)

David Looked to the Sacred Cities, God's Presence was Gone

David looked to the sacred cities, Mount Moriah and Mount Zion, where God's presence had once dwelt. But he realized that the **presence of God** was gone, (it had lifted). Both places were known by the Hebrew people as places to worship. But those places were now in disrepair and no longer in use.

David said, "now I know that my help comes from the Lord, the Maker of Heaven and Earth." Because the Lord is never limited to a geographic area. Worship and intercession are not about being in a specific geographic location. But they are about right attitude of heart and the place of encountering God.

As we enter into times of prayer, intercession and spiritual warfare, it is important to know that the Lord is your keeper and your protector. Psalm 121 finishes with an awesome description of how the Lord is watching over us. This scripture declares: He is your keeper, He is your shade, He protects you and He keeps your soul. The Lord guards you as you are coming in and going out (real every day life).

Psalm 121:5, 7-8

> 5 The LORD is **your keeper**; the LORD is your shade on your right hand.

> 7 The LORD will **protect you** from all evil;
> He will keep your soul.

> 8 The LORD **will guard** your going out and your coming in from this time forth and forever.

His Presence was Given to Help Us do Spiritual Warfare

There is no **greater help** than when His power and His person are released in our worship and prayer. When we do it, passionate prayer opens spiritual gateways ascending into Heaven. The depths of worship is a tool and weapon of priesthood that flows with **spiritual might** on it. The heart of intercession (breaking the darkness) has **His authority** on it. Intercessory prayer has the power to **bind and loose** as Jesus said in the Gospels.

Luke 10:17-20

> ^{17} The seventy returned with joy, saying,
>> "Lord, even the demons are subject to us in Your name."
> ^{18} And He said to them,
>> "I was watching satan fall from heaven like lightning.
>
> ^{19} Behold, I have given you **authority** to tread on serpents
>> and scorpions, and **over all** the power of **the enemy**,
>> and nothing will injure you.
> ^{20} Nevertheless do not rejoice in this,
>> that spirits are subject to you,
>> but rejoice that your names are recorded in heaven."

The Authority of the Crucified Lamb and Victorious Lion

Most human beings will seldom walk in a place of true authority. We have been trained to wait for someone else's approval or permission before venturing out to do almost anything.

With Jesus, real authority comes from Who He is as the King of Glory, what He has done as the Crucified Lamb, and His place as the Victorious Lion. Our inheritance is to take our place in Him with His authority to do intercession full of blessing and spiritual warfare like Jesus does. His presence gives us real power and authority.

Matthew 28:16-18

> ^{16} But the eleven disciples proceeded to Galilee,
>> to the mountain which Jesus had designated.
> ^{17} When they saw Him, **they worshipped Him**;

but some were doubtful.

[18] And Jesus came up and spoke to them, saying,
*"**All authority** has been given to Me in*
heaven and on earth."

A Clear Type of a Warring Worshipper

As you let the high praises of God stay in your mouth and release the power of the two-edged sword in your hand, you become a **warring worshipper**. People who do passionate worship and corporate prayer become fairly militant about it and stay very committed to it. It is because they have learned that singing and praying the Word of God releases His promises and starts the flow of His blessing.

The principles found in Psalm 149 help us understand spiritual warfare. Real worship and prayer released at their highest levels, begin to inhibit and interfere with the dominion of the demonic kingdom.

As we do spiritual warfare with God's holy power, the judgment that has already been written by the hand of God is being executed against the kingdom of darkness as we pray.

Streaming in Heaven's Flow

The High Praises of God in Our Mouth

The Two-Edged Sword in Our Hand

This is the honor for all His Godly Ones:
The power of worship and prayer
releases justice and judgment.

I. The Power of the Simplest Songs

When you go back through human history . . . You find the simplest songs are life changing, load bearing and have the power to carry the human soul through the darkest of hours.

A. Negro Spirituals are Christian songs, most of them concern what the Bible says and how to live with (in) the Spirit of God. These songs carried the African slaves through the length and breadth of one of the darkest hours of human history.

II. The High Praises of God

The high praises of God were simple songs that the Hebrew people sang. They are full of what we now know as the canonized Word of God. Simple word phrases were put to simple melodies and used for powerful worship to God.

A. People from denominational backgrounds during the Charismatic Renewal learned the Word of God more in depth because they were singing these scripture songs. It was a worship, song movement that went around the world in less than 20 years.

III. Spontaneous Songs and Songs of the Moment

A. Songs in worship created on the spot while flowing in His presence has been a large part of my life from the very beginning of my worship leading.

In the very beginning we had waves of worship and the presence of God came through our meetings. I have always viewed it as the grace of God that would help us plumb the depths of deeper worship.

155

B. Here are a few dimensions of the high praises of God.

1) Everyone has a choice: by your will to enter in to the stream of God or to not enter in.

2) There is an understanding that songs and music are a large part of doing high praises. We use music as one of the weapons in our arsenal.

3) All the singers and musicians are open to flowing in the Holy Spirit and operating in the presence of God as our base and foundation.

IV. Two-Edged Sword in Our Hands

Let the high praises of God be in their mouth, and then, in a holy zeal for His honor, let them take a two-edged sword in their hand, to fight His battles against the enemies of His kingdom.

A. Psalm 144:1 goes hand in hand with Psalm 149:6.

They both speak of the warfare theme and of what God has put in our hands. I have always viewed my voice, my guitar, my hands and my piano as extensions of my life and heart. Further, I see them as consecrated, dedicated weapons made ready for God's use.

B. Psalm 144:1 - *Blessed be the LORD, my rock, Who trains my hands for war, and my fingers for battle;*

Psalm 149:6 - *Let the **high praises** of God be in their mouth, and a **two-edged sword** in their hand,*

C. The holy zeal for the Lord's honor; the more we commit our time and energy to worship, prayer and music, our times of encountering God will grow and expand.

V. Operating in the Spiritual Realm

A. When we are singing and praying the Word of God, the written Word is judgment in and of itself. It is enough to overpower evil and triumph over darkness.

B. Passionate prayer opens spiritual gateways ascending into Heaven. The depths of worship is a tool and weapon of priesthood that flows with spiritual might on it.

Urgency! Take Heed, Watch and Pray

Prayer always brings light and illumination.
Jesus said, "Do not be troubled,
only have a pray-full spirit."
So we take heed, watch and pray,
because of Jesus' counsel.
In light of it all
"I say to all: Watch!"

Awake, O sleeper. Up! thou sleeper,
Wake up from your sleep,
Climb out of your coffins;
Christ shall shine (make day dawn)
upon you and give you (show) you light.

Chapter Ten

Urgency! Take Heed, Watch and Pray

Be Circumspect, (looking), Praying and Be Devout because you don't know when the Lord will be returning.

Mark 13:32-37 No One Knows the Day or the Hour

³² *But of that day and hour no one knows, not even the angels in heaven, nor the Son, but only the Father.*

³³ ***Take heed, watch and pray;*** *for you do not know when the time is.*
Be on your guard [constantly alert], and watch and pray; for you do not know when the time will come. (AMP)

*Be **circumspect**, be **vigilant**, and **devout**: because you are uncertain when that time will be.* (Mace NT)

³⁴ *It is like a man going to a far country, who left his house and gave authority to his servants, and to each his work, and commanded the doorkeeper to watch.*

³⁵ ***Watch therefore, for you do not know when the master of the house is coming --*** *in the evening, at midnight, at the crowing of the rooster, or in the morning,*

³⁶ *lest, coming suddenly, he find you sleeping.*

³⁷ *And what I say to you, **I say to all: Watch!***

In the gospel of Mark, the thirteenth chapter, there is a tremendous unfolding of revelation on the elements of the sign of the times and the end of the age. When will these things happen and what are the signs?   (Mark 13:1-5)

The importance of prayer, **staying alert** (which is in every believer's ability to do daily) and the power of seeing is magnified in light of Jesus' words. **Take heed, watch and pray!!** These three things keep us in fresh oil and on track so we can be prepared (ready) for the time that is coming and even more so His second coming. Now let's define each one of these.

Take Heed

"Take heed," starts for me with a military and police term "your head should be on a swivel." It is referring to walking around with 360 degree vision and sensitivity. I am amazed with the number of people who are caught off guard many times a week by things that are taking place around them. They haven't even noticed them. In other words, they don't know **what** is going on around them.

The phrase, "**take heed**" is defined like this:

These are more about the natural eye:

- ❖ to see, discern, as with the bodily eye
- ❖ to have and use the **power** of **seeing**
- ❖ to **turn the eyes** to anything; to look at or upon, gaze at

These are more about spiritual or mentally seeing:

- ❖ to have (the power of) understanding
- ❖ to discern mentally, (spiritually) perceive, **discover**
- ❖ to consider, contemplate, to weigh carefully, examine

Active prayer and intercession
opens and increases
the realm of our seeing
and makes available
higher grade spiritual vision.

There is one other dimension of taking heed that is really powerful. In a geographical sense of places, mountains, buildings, etc. it means **turning towards** any quarter or facing it.

Prayer and devotion give us a greater ability to "turn toward any quarter." We can face things head on in prayer and worship that otherwise we may avoid or run away from. This is why a greater dedication to prayer is so important.

Watch

"Watch" should be more readily understood by each one us. If you drive a car, if you ride a bike, or if you go running in the morning or evening, you had better be watching. If not, an accident is sure to happen.

The phrase "**to watch**" is defined like this:

These are more about staying awake and being attentive:

- ❖ to keep awake, attentive, ready
- ❖ to be circumspect, prudent, **guarded**
- ❖ to exercise constant vigilance over something
  [drawn from the image of the (good) shepherd]

These are more about alertness :

- ❖ a wakeful frame of mind, as opposed to listlessness
- ❖ signifies the state untouched by slumber,
  or beclouding influences . . .

These definitions can be used in our prayer times. Right now in our Prayer Room, one of the major topics we are praying about is "Awakening." If we are watching, we will be able to discern the current sleeping state of the Church. We will feel the need to intercede for our own awakening and the church itself.

The whole element of "watching" opens the door for us to start moving into greater awakening. Literally, these definitions should work their way into our vocabulary for prayer. We should mark this in our memory, that our prayers are rising like incense before the Lord. Our prayers, worship and intercession is effecting change both in time and in the spirit dimension.

Ephesians 5:14

> For this reason He says, **"Awake, sleeper,**
> and arise from the dead, and Christ will **shine on you."**

160

Therefore He says ,
Awake, O sleeper. Up! thou sleeper,
Wake up from your sleep,
Climb out of your coffins;
Christ shall shine (make day dawn)
upon you and give you (show) you light.

(MSG)

Pray

The phrase "**to pray**" is defined like this:

This is as simple as talking to the Lord. Most prayer is offered in faith because you believe that God is bigger than your situation or the things that you are praying over and about.

Pray - be devout - to throw or to **pour forth words** or sounds; to pour out prayers

❖ to bless . . . to preach . . . to intercede . . . to intervene
❖ to pour forth water, as in a violent rain
   (Prayer should have this kind of energy on it and in it.)
❖ to supplicate good; entreat or urge
❖ to ask with earnestness or zeal, as for a favor or something desirable

Prayer within worship means to supplicate, implore; to ask with true reverence and humility.

Devout: yielding a **reverential attention** to God; with ardent (heart-felt) devotion to the Lord.

Four Prayer Truths

There are four prayer truths found in Mark 13. Each one is full of God's provision and saving grace.

First truth - Prayer brings light and illumination.

Second truth - Do not be troubled, only have a pray-full spirit.

Third truth - Take heed, watch and pray.

Fourth truth - Jesus' counsel in light of it all
   "I say to all: Watch!"

The First Prayer Truth - **Prayer Brings Light and Illumination**

Prayer is a way of consistently asking and receiving from the vault of His wisdom. Keeping an ongoing conversation with the Lord daily is an important part of a believer's walk.

Taking heed is important because it brings light and illumination and keeps us in a place where we are actively aware and flowing in the Holy Spirit. It would be so much harder to catch a band of believers off guard who are praying together. Do individual prayer, but fire up even more in corporate prayer.

Mark 13:1-5   *Many will come in My name, saying, `I am He!' and will mislead many.*

¹ *Then as He went out of the temple, one of His disciples said to Him, "Teacher, see what manner of stones and what buildings are here!"*

² *And Jesus answered and said to him, "Do you see these great buildings? Not one stone shall be left upon another, that shall not be thrown down."*

³ *Now as He sat on the Mount of Olives opposite the temple, Peter, James, John, and Andrew*
asked Him privately, *(a prayer truth)*

⁴ *"Tell us,* **when** *will these things be?* (Question #1)

And **what** *will be* **the sign** *when all these things will be fulfilled?"* (Question #2)

⁵ *And Jesus, answering them, began to say:*
*"**Take heed** that no one deceives you."*

Most everyone is concerned about the subject, "the last days." People that know the Lord and people that could care less are still sensing some imminent, catastrophic event concerning the future. But the point here is **to be praying**. There is so much power in corporate prayer as we come together in the Prayer Room. It is energizing and it is keeping us in a place to hear the voice of the Lord.

Next Jesus gives the disciples His counsel by saying, "be careful that no one deceives you." Anytime Jesus gives us counsel, we want to pay close attention to that and make the most of what He is saying.

The Second Prayer Truth -
Do Not be Troubled, Only Have a Pray-full Spirit

This is quite a statement from Jesus for us to have to adhere to. Do not be troubled is a tall order for most of us because our day is full of pits and potholes of anxiety and change. The way to truly defeat it though is to have a **pray-full** spirit. This is why praying throughout the day has its own merits for as we meet troubles, we can solve and overcome them.

Mark 13:7, 9-11, 13

> [7] *But when you hear of wars and rumors of wars,*
> > ***do not be troubled****; (only have a **pray-full spirit***)
> > *for such things must happen, but the end is not yet.*

> [9] *But **watch out** for yourselves, for they will deliver you up to councils, and you will be beaten in the synagogues.*
> *You will be brought [stand] before rulers and kings for My sake, **for a testimony** to them.*
> [10] *And the gospel must first be preached to all the nations.*
> [11] *But when they arrest you and deliver you up, do not worry beforehand, or premeditate what you will speak.*
>
> *But whatever is given you in that hour, speak that; for it is not you who speak, **but the Holy Spirit** (speaks).*

> [13] *And you will be hated by all for My name's sake.*
> ***But he who endures** to the end shall be saved.*

Thank the Lord the scripture (verse 7) records that we have a safe haven in Him where we can deal with troubles. If you become a person that is pray-full, full of prayer, your ability to weather storms and hard times will be so much greater.

Enduring strength is the secret to longevity in the realm of faithfulness. The power of prayer imparts strength by its very nature.

Prayer is what gives us strength to stand in the place of long-term endurance. So many people view prayer as energy draining and somewhat exhausting. Prayer always lifts the spirit even in the heat of intense times of intercession. There are elements of prayer that always bring refreshing.

The Third Prayer Truth - **Take Heed, Watch and Pray**

Jesus said we must do this, the "take heed, watch and pray" lifestyle. This command covers the whole of the Body of Christ, every one should be in a place where they are on their guard (AMP). We are going to be watching, on the alert (NAS) wakeful and praying (GLT). Let's get busy doing what Jesus said.

Mark 13:32-34

> [32] *But of that day and hour no one knows, not even the angels in heaven, nor the Son, but only the Father.*
>
> [33] ***Take heed, watch and pray;***
>   *for you do not know when the time is.*
> [34] *It is like a man going to a far country, who left his house and* ***gave authority*** *to his servants, and to each his work, and commanded the doorkeeper to watch.*

Here's what Matthew Henry's Commentary says about Mark 13.

["As to both, your duty is to *watch and pray.*
Therefore the time (of His return) is kept a secret, that you may be engaged to stand always upon your guard. *Take ye heed* of every thing that would **indispose you** for your Master's coming, and would render your accounts (at a loss) and your spirit *perplexed,* so too.

Watch for His coming, that it may not at any time be a surprise to you, and *pray* for that grace which is necessary to qualify you for it. For *ye know not when the time is;* and you are concerned to be ready for that *every day,* which may come *any day."*]

Prayer is the communication source from God to us for our hearing, discerning and seeing more clearly. That is why our commitment to doing what Jesus said is so important. I am excited that Jesus gave us a way forward while we are waiting for Him to come back again.

TAKE HEED, START WATCHING AND KEEP PRAYING.

The Fourth Prayer Truth -
Jesus' counsel in light of it all "I say to all: Watch!"

Active in prayer: guarantees we won't be found sleeping, but watching.

Mark 13:35-37

> [35] **Watch therefore**, *for you do not know when the master of the house is coming-- in the evening, at midnight,*
>> *at the crowing of the rooster, or in the morning--*
> [36] *lest, coming suddenly, he find you sleeping.*
> [37] *And what I say to you, **I say to all: Watch!***

The real urgency in this time is to be ready for the Second Coming of Christ. He is coming again. The "day of the Lord" is coming soon. Time, as we understand it, will not go on forever. There is coming the "End of the Age."

Eschatology is the study of the End Times. There are volumes of books and study of this subject including the massive, awesome book of Revelation. These books surely give us all a real sense of spiritual urgency to be obedient and ready.

Pressing more into prayer, worship, and intercession helps us to be more keenly aware of His times and seasons. The element of devotion to Jesus helps keep us stable in the most troubled times. At the same time it is keeping us in a ready-state for the day and the hour of the Lord. We can sense as we spend time with the Lord that there is a real urgency!

The Day of the Lord . . . like a thief in the night

I Thessalonians 5:1-6

> [1] *Now as to the **times** and the **epochs**, brethren, you have no need of anything to be written to you.*
> [2] *For you yourselves know full well that the day of the Lord will come just **like a thief in the night**.*
> [3] *While they are saying, "Peace and safety!" then (sudden) destruction will come upon them suddenly like labor pains upon a woman with child, and **they will not escape**.*

*⁴ But you, brethren, **are not in darkness**, that the day would overtake you like a thief;*

*⁵ for you are all **sons of light** and **sons of day**. We are not of night nor of darkness;*

*⁶ so then let us not sleep as others (the remaining ones) do, but **let us be** alert (watch) and sober (self-controlled).*

Let every person tremble. Let every believer walk in the fear of the Lord for this is as high level as you can get concerning Jesus coming again. The Apostle Paul in the New Testament does not mince any words on how the day of the Lord is coming: like a thief in the night. These elements about the Lord coming back again are truly awesome and unchangeable.

But Paul tells these believers, you are not in darkness that the day will overtake you as a thief because you are sons of light and sons of the day. We are no longer of the night or the darkness. Hip hip hurray and Hallelujah! This is such a powerful confirmation of our new life in Christ.

(2 Corinthians 5:17 - we are new creatures in Christ Jesus)

So here is what Paul said we should all do, let us not sleep as others do, but let us be alert (watch) and let us be sober (self-controlled). We are literally surrounded by these words. I want to continue being strong in the Lord and the power of His might. I want to finish strong and fulfill my godly destiny for Him. But now I know, the only way to do that is to take heed, watch and pray.

For the Lord Himself will Descend from Heaven

I Thessalonians 4:16-18

*¹⁶ For the **Lord Himself** will **descend** from **heaven** with a shout, [a cry of command], with the voice of the archangel and with the trumpet of God, and the dead in Christ will rise first.*

¹⁷ Then we who are alive and remain will be caught up together with them in the clouds to meet the Lord in the air, and so we shall always be with the Lord.

¹⁸ Therefore comfort one another with these words.

Verse 16 clearly tells us how the Lord is coming back, not when but how. This is a great scripture to meditate on. It is found in five knowable parts.

For the **Lord Himself**

- ❖ will descend from heaven (for all to see)

- ❖ with a shout, [a cry of command], (for all to hear)

- ❖ with the voice of the archangel and (for all to know)

- ❖ with the trumpet of God, (sound of a heavenly instrument)

- ❖ and the dead in Christ will rise first. (the sure end result)

These are the distinct signs that the Lord has come again. Our point today is that the more we are praying and involved in worship, the more sensitive our spirit will be in tune with the times. I found very few churches are intentionally walking out this "take heed, watch and pray" command from Jesus. The Prayer Room by its very nature, is fulfilling all three. It keeps us on our toes spiritually and keeps our minds focused on the Lord.

Life is Urgent

Luke 9:60-62

[60] *Jesus … "First things first. Your business is life, not death. And* ***life is urgent****: announce God's kingdom!"*
[61] *Then another said, "I'm ready to follow you, Master, but first excuse me while I get things straightened out at home."*
[62] *Jesus said, "No* ***procrastination.*** *No backward looks. You can't put God's kingdom off till tomorrow.* ***Seize the day."*** *(MSG)*

Take heed, watch and pray is **how** we seize the day. All of life really is urgent. There is so much going on in everyone's life continually that we must use intercession and worship as anchor point. So pray more and worship more. And when you are finished doing that, pray more and worship more again.

Streaming in Heaven's Flow

Urgency! Take Heed, Watch and Pray

Be circumspect, praying and be devout.

Mark 13:32 - 37   No One Knows the Day or the Hour

I. The Importance of Prayer and Staying Alert

Every believer has the ability to do this daily, stay alert. The power of prayer is magnified in light of Jesus' words.

A. Take Heed

1) Take heed is a military term that means "your head should be on a swivel." It is referring to walking around with 360 degree vision and sensitivity.

2) Take heed - to **turn the eyes** to anything; to look at or upon, gaze at, as with the natural eye; to discern mentally, (spiritually) perceive, **discover**,

    Active prayer and intercession opens and increases the realm of our seeing and makes available higher grade spiritual vision.

B. Watch

If we are watching, we will be able to discern the current sleeping state of the Church. We will feel the need to intercede for our own awakening and the church itself.

1) Watch - about staying awake and being attentive; to be circumspect, prudent, guarded; to exercise vigilance.

2) Alertness - signifies the state untouched by slumber, or beclouding influences

    Through taking heed and watching, our prayers continue to rise like incense before the Lord. Our worship and intercession is effecting change both in time and in the spirit dimension.

    *Therefore He says , Awake, O sleeper. Up! thou sleeper, Wake up from your sleep, **Climb out** of your **coffins;** Christ shall shine (make day dawn) upon you and give you (show) you light.* (MSG)

168

C. Pray - to pour forth words or sounds;
consequently, to pour out prayers.

Prayer starts with being devout, maintaining the fear of the Lord or reverential awe toward God.

1) Pray - To bless, to intercede, but in such a manner as to pour forth water, as in a violent rain.
Prayer should have this kind of energy.

2) To supplicate: (entreat or urge) To ask with zeal earnestness, as for a favor or something desirable.

II. Four Prayer Truths

Each one is full of God's provision and saving grace.

A. Prayer brings light and illumination.

Prayer is a way of consistently asking and receiving from the vault of His wisdom. Keeping an ongoing conversation with the Lord daily is an important part of a believer's walk.

B. Do not be troubled, only have a pray-full spirit.

The power of prayer imparts strength by its very nature. I read this scripture and say, "I will have a pray-full spirit and a spirit full of prayer."

C. Take heed, watch and pray.

Jesus' command covers the whole of the Body of Christ, every one in a place where they are on their guard (AMP). We are going to be watching, on the alert (NAS) wakeful and praying (GLT). Let's stay busy doing what Jesus said.

D. Jesus' counsel in light of it all "I say to all: **Watch!**"

III. Life is Urgent

Luke 9: 60 *Jesus ... "First things first. Your business is life, not death. And **life is urgent**: Announce God's kingdom!"*

Take heed, watch and pray is **how** we seize the day. There is so much going on in everyone's life continually that we must use intercession and worship as anchor point. So pray more and worship more. And when you are finished doing that, pray more and worship more again.

The Top Twenty Reasons Why Most Christians do not Pray

I think all of us have heard every excuse in the book about why people do not pray or do not pray more. It is so self-defeating to not at least try to find your way to a greater intimacy with the Lord Jesus.

The great conqueror Joshua said "as for me and my house, we will serve the Living God," and we should be saying, "as for me and my house we will worship and pray to the Living God."

No Time and Too Busy:

1) I'm just way too busy. My work schedule is more than I can handle right now.

2) Lack of time: I can't seem to keep track of my time.

3) Prayer is so boring; I find it a waste of time compared to the Internet and watching TV.

4) It's not a top priority for me; I have more important things to do.

5) I need to get proper sleep and that is so much more important.

Lazy, Undisciplined, Fear of Failure:

6) I don't really know how to pray so I don't have any confidence that I'll get answers.

7) My whole life is so undisciplined, I couldn't even consider a daily prayer time.

8) Honestly, I'm just too lazy.

9) I have a real fear of failing in prayer, and I don't know how to start.

10) I think prayer seems like a whole lot of work for so little return.

God does not Hear or Answer My Prayers:

11) I am not sure if God would hear my prayers because of my current or past sin problems.

12) I am not sure if God would answer my prayers, because I'm not sure I have enough faith.

13) I just don't believe that God really cares. Look at the evil that is in this world.

14) I have never seen time in prayer bear much fruit. My friends have prayed and not much has changed.

15) I know that other people are praying for me so I hope that's enough.

Stressed Out, Overlooked and Overloaded:

16) I am way too stressed out; I am so overloaded I can't think straight.

17) I feel that I am overlooked by most people and no one has invited me to pray.

18) Procrastination: I will do it tomorrow or the next day.

19) I de-stress and get my relief from drinking, smoking and occasional drug use.

20) Something is always coming up in my life and schedule that keeps me from prayer and getting the Prayer Room.

What do these 20 things have in common?

It's all about **me** . . . and not much about Jesus.

Everyone Has Time to Pray: Here's Why

24 hrs. a day times 7 days a week =	**168** hours
Sleep 8 hrs. times 7 days =	- **56** hours
	112 hours left

Work and related commute =	- **48** hours
	64 hours left

Eating and preparing to eat
(30 min. breakfasts - 3.5 hrs.)
(45 min. lunches - 5.25 hrs.)
(One hour dinners -7 hrs) =15.75 hrs. -**16** hours
48 hours left

Family time: (one hour per	
week night, 6 hours on weekend)	- **11** hours
	37 hours left

Work around the house (10 hrs.)	- **10** hours
	27 hours left

Church twice a week - (5hrs.)	- **5** hours
	22 hours left

Exercise, Hobby, TV (1.5 hrs. a day)	-**11** hours
	11 hours left

Devotion: 30 minutes a day - 3.5 hrs.	- **4** hours
	7 hours left

---

7 hours left - for one night of prayer a week or
for one morning of prayer a week
[**2 hours a week**, plus drive time]

Made in the USA
San Bernardino, CA
22 February 2014